MOTORING

by

Brian J Deller.

Especially written for English speaking residents and visitors to Spain who own, rent or operate cars and motorcycles in Spain.

Published by the Author.

DISCLAIMER.

This book is intended as a guide for the English speaking visitor to, or resident in, Spain to assist them in quickly becoming acquainted with the driving and owning of a private motor vehicle in Spain, including rental cars and motorcycles.   It is not intended to be used as a reference book for litigation. The author stresses that if / when needed, professional legal advice is sought.   The contents of this book cannot be used as a basis for any claim against the author or any other party associated with it.

First printed February 2004.

Copyright © September, 2003 Brian John Deller.

ISBN 84-607-9617-5

Design and layout by the author. Published by the author.

Grateful thanks to Hendrik (Henti) Eksteen for his help with negotiations. Also the legal help as listed on page 4.

Printed in Spain by: -
 P. R. Grafis, Fuengirola, Malaga, Spain. Tel. (0034) 952 66 77 88
 E-mail prgrafis@prgrafis.es

MA Deposito Legal   MA 1508-2004

Author's E-mail address, **viadevida@spainvia.com**

MOTORING IN SPAIN.

ntroduction.

iis book is a quick reference facility for all English-speaking people operating a car or motor-cycle in)ain, especially in the holiday areas on the Southern and Eastern Coasts where many either live or sit.   There are other books available in Spain with information on motoring Laws but they lack the ick reference facility that this book gives, especially the useful translations and **road signs** all in one t of covers. For this reason, the book is designed to be **easy to carry in a car glove compartment with a motorcycle** (moto).   As a point of interest, a survey by the author showed that many reigners who have lived here for years, and even some Spanish friends, are ignorant of what many of e road signs actually mean, as well as many of the Laws.   This is probably the same in many)untries, and Spain (and the Continent) has many more signs than, for example, the UK and Ireland.

is not intended to be a fully comprehensive "driving lesson manual".   Some minor repetition of formation is deliberate to get a needed message through or to save having to jump from page to ige (something the author hates in other reference books).

2001, Spain was statistically the third worst country in the EU for deaths due to road related ccidents, and more recent figures show an increase in deaths.   An important thought to keep in mind.

addition to a summary of the rules and regulations concerning driving in Spain, this book contains)mmon words and phrases translated into Spanish and vice-versa, including for an emergency such ; an accident, or for buying spare parts or organising repairs where English is not spoken. Many of e words are not in the usual small tourist guides and dictionaries.

he book is **not** to be considered as a reference book to support any litigation concerning motoring fences. Any such specific legal inquiries and other needs should be referred to a Spanish specialist wyer (*abogado*) or legal / business advisor (*gestor*), etc.

rian Deller, Malaga
ecember, 2003

For updates and other new information, visit our web site at: -

www.spainvia.com/motoringinspain.htm

E-mail, **bjdeller@spainvia.com**

The author thanks the following two professionals who have checked the legal and general statements made in this book.

They are: -

Don Jose Luis Martinez Hens, *Abogado* (lawyer).

Jose has a legal practice with offices based in Fuengirola and Periana on the Costa del Sol. Jose spent a year working in the USA, and he then returned to Spain. His year in the US means that he is fully fluent in English and familiar with US laws, and being qualified in Spain, he is experienced in all types of Spanish legal matters including motoring litigation. Jose checked the legal matters in the book and advised any changes where necessary.

Office 1.   Calle Capitan 12, Local 4, 29640 Fuengirola, Malaga, Spain
Tel. / Fax. (0034) 952 47 09 19.
Office 2.   Carretera Torreblance del Mar, 12, 29710 Periana, Malaga.
Tel. / Fax. (0034) 952 53 65 13
Mob. 600-706-044.   E-Mail, JLMHENS@terra.es

Don Ricardo Bocanegra Sanchez, *Abogado* and *Gestor*.

In Spain, much work is carried out by trained and certificated professional specialists called **gestors** who are well versed in the Law and in business matters. Working in an office called a **gestoria**, the *gestor* is available to carry out all the tasks that are necessary for the average Spanish citizen and foreign resident or visitor, who needs legal administrative matters carried out as referred to in this book.   **Gestoria Bocanegra**, with a staff of over ten people, is one of the largest such offices in Marbella. Ricardo, a highly qualified lawyer, has checked and advised on the aspects of this book covered by his area of expertise.

Ricardo and his staff are fluent in English and their knowledge is at your service.

Gestoria Bocanegra, Avenida Ricardo Soriano 65, 2nd Floor,
(OCASO Building), 29600 Marbella.
Tel. (0034) 952 77 58 35 Fax (0034) 952 82 99 32.
E-Mail, bocanegra@marbella.net

The author, Brian J Deller.

Brian Deller is of the age where he has qualified for the UK State pension, but he finds retirement too boring, so this book has been compiled to satisfy the real need for it in Spain.

Joining the RAF as an aircraft-apprentice at the age of 16, after finding out he was colour-blind and could not take up flying, he served for thirteen years specialising in aircraft engines of all types. This was followed by three years with Rolls-Royce Aero-Engines, mainly in the USA, until that company went into liquidation in 1970/1. He then spent five years with earthmoving equipment manufacturer JCB, for whom he travelled, especially the Far East, Australia & New Zealand, working on dealer-development. Brian was offered employment in 1975 during a business visit to South Africa, and he and his family moved there in 1976, staying until 1999, as by then, the terrible crime situation there made everyday a dangerous existence.

There, he also did a lot of voluntary charity work amongst which was the training of motorcyclists of all ages on how to ride safely, a task he had previously done with the RAC-ACU scheme in the UK. Some "students" had been riding for years, some were just starting and others were local council traffic-police motorcyclists for whom official training did not exist at that time. Two years were spent as a police reservist where, working with the after effects following serious road accidents (including personally advising relatives of deaths), again showed him the lack of good sense that many of us seem to practice as far as driving is concerned, especially driving drunk or "drugged".

Spain was chosen as the "escape" destination in 1999 because Brian's wife Beverley had often visited this country as a child and loved the Spanish way of life, and Brian agreed after two flying visits. This book has been written as a result of his experiences driving here, and the accepted fact that most foreign visitors and residents are ignorant of the many motoring differences here, especially the road signs; even many of those who have lived here for ten years or more.

Brian has over thirty-six years of motor insurance no-claims bonuses despite riding (and racing) high-speed motor-cycles, and driving a wide variety of cars in several countries.

For up-dated information since printing, or to advise any of your comments or suggestions, please go to our Website: -

www.spainvia.com/motoringinspain.htm

Part No.	Contents	Page No.

Part 1 - 1

Definitions and General Information.

Please note that age limits refer to Spanish licence regulations only.

Driver (*Conductor / a*). The person who is in control or responsible for the vehicle, including those "animal-powered", while on the public highways, even when not in motion.

Pedestrian (*Peatón / ona*). A person who uses the public highway, including footpaths, while on foot. These users are subject to the same Laws as all road users, and include those who are pushing non-motorised vehicles such as baby-carriages, etc.

Vehicle Ownership and Insurance Documents. If visiting Spain in your vehicle, your normal proof of ownership papers should be carried at all times in the vehicle. If you are driving a Spanish registration plated vehicle, including a rental vehicle where the papers should be supplied by the rental company (in the glove compartment?), you should carry: -

⇒   **A. *Permiso de Circulación*.** Shows the registered owner of the vehicle.

⇒   **B**. The certificate of insurance issued by the insurance company (also known as the **Green Card?**).

⇒   **C.** For Spanish registered cars, if the vehicle is more than four years old (two years for service vehicles, taxis and rental cars), it must have been tested for roadworthiness (**ITV**, in UK, **MOT**), with the test sticker receipt on the upper right side of the windscreen. For motorcycles, the "free period" is five years (unless they are used for rentals), the test is then needed every two years. See **Part 5 - 2** for more details. The date (month/year) of the next due test date is noted on the sticker. Commercial vehicles have a free period of two years, and then are tested every year. **If a foreign vehicle, it must conform to the testing procedures of the country of origin and have the certificate for same with the vehicle.**

⇒ The ***Tarjeta de Inspeccion Technica de Vehiculos*** (legal technical specification of the car, as supplied by the EU licensed manufacturer).

⇒ You should also carry the standard accident report form, the ***declaración amistosa de accidente de automóvil*** ("agreed statement of facts on a motor vehicle accident"). If involved in an accident, the details can be legally binding in Court if signed by all drivers involved in an accident. The details must be correct in this standard form, which is issued by most EU insurance companies in various languages, before signing it so it is important that you know what it says.

AN ENGLISH TRANSLATION OF THIS FORM IS AT THE BACK OF THIS BOOK.

⇒ **Driving Licence (*permiso de conducción*).** If you are driving a Spanish registered vehicle **owned by you, you must have a Spanish driving licence**. It is a simple procedure to obtain one by using your current EU licence as described in the section of this book on driving licences. The fine is up to €.400 for not doing so. Your photo-card licence issued in the UK is legally acceptable as long as it is current and is for the vehicle being driven for a stay up to six months, including the expiry date being **after** you intend to leave Spain. Non-EU citizens must have an **International Driver's Licence** issued in their home country. Check the glove-box of your rental car for other needed documents described above while on the road in Spain. If you are resident in Spain, you may obtain a Spanish licence without "losing" the British document and the Spanish licence is OK to use anywhere in the EU. (See also **Part 6-4** for more information).

<u>VEHICLE DEFINITIONS</u>.

The following descriptions are of the various vehicle classifications with limitations, as covered on the Spanish Driving Permit/Licence. Most here will not be driven by foreigners unless they are in commercial business and will be advised by a local specialist, but they are included for your information. The Spanish "driving licence classification" (DLC) is noted in brackets, ie (DLC—D1)

Please note that the following listed classifications applies to the intended readers of this book. There are many more that are specialist and commercial not shown here as they would not normally apply to a foreign visitor or even foreign resident. Mopeds, scooters and small cars (2 or 3 wheels) with engines not bigger than 49 cc with a designed maximum speed of not more than 45 kph (28 mph) may be driven by car licence-holders and do not need the requisite licence for that class of vehicle. Note the minimum ages though.

⟹ **Bicycle (*Bicicleta*).** Non-motorised bicycles or three-wheeler. (No Class).

⟹ **Moped (*Ciclo*). 50 cc** motorised bicycle with pedals. Maximum designed speed of 45 kph (28 mph), engine power 0,5 kw. Also a four-wheel machine, less than 350 kg in weight and up to 50 cc/4 kw capacity/rated engine power. 14 years old minimum to ride, 16 with a passenger. (DLC-A1).

⟹ **Light car (*Cuadriciclio ligero*).** Maximum weight 350 kg. (not incl. batteries if electrical power). Max speed 45 kph (28 mph). Engine 50 cc / 4 kw. (DLC-A1)

⟹ **Scooter (*Moto*).** A two-wheeled motorised vehicle. The most modern smaller scooters and mopeds are equipped with automatic gearing, which makes riding easier and safer; just open the throttle and go. Minimum age 14 yrs. for up to 49 cc engine size: 50 cc to 124 cc, 16 yrs: over 125 cc to a power of 25 kw, 18 years. Over 25 kw, 20 years is the minimum age for a licence. (DLC-A1 & A)

⟹ **Three-wheeled vehicle.** Usually a small "city" vehicle with a <u>minimum</u> power to weight ratio of 0,11 kw to 100 kg. Min. age 16 yrs. (DLC-A1)

⟹ **Motorcycles up to 125 cc/11 kw. (DLC-A1)**

⟹ **Motorcycles up to 25 kw (34 hp) engine power or 0,16 kw per kilogramme unladen weight.** (DLC-A)

⟹ **Motorcycles over 25 kw**, including with a sidecar. Min. age 18 yrs. plus two year's previous experience. (DLC-A).**a)** **4-Wheel motorcycle**. If electric, battery weight not included. Gross maximum weight for sport 400 kg: if commercial, 550 kg. Maximum power 15 kw. (DLC-A)

Please do not forget that updates are on our web site.

⇒ **Cars and light trucks/vans up to 3.500 kg**. Includes most motor-cars: this is the commonest classification of licence. Minimum age 18 yrs. (DLC-B)

⇒ **Commercial non-articulated,** over 3.500 kg up to 7.500 kg. (DLC-C1)

⇒ **Up to 16 seat passenger plus driver vehicle,** public service driver's permit (PSV) needed if used for hire with driver. (DLC-D1)

⇒ **Local Coach or Omnibus** (50 km radius), PSV permit needed. (DLC-D)

⇒ **Car towing** a trailer/caravan. Maximum speed 80 kph (49 mph) (DLC-B)

⇒ **Commercial vehicle** towing a trailer up to 750 kg gross weight, maximum vehicle all up weight 12.000 kg. (DLC-C1)

Other vehicles include trolley buses, two-decker buses, and vehicles not normally driven by foreigners unless they are especially tested as drivers.

Further Spanish licence and other documentation regulations are in **Part 6-4**.

You will see vehicles with a small white sign with "**SP**" on it in black lettering. This indicates "*Servicio Publico*", and shows that the vehicle is used for hire and transportation of paying customers.

TYPES OF ROADS. (MORE DETAILS IN PART 7, SIGNS).

- A *CALLE* and an *AVENIDA* are **roads/streets/avenues**, where normally, there are speed limits of **50 kph** (31 mph), unless otherwise posted, usually at **20 kph** (12 mph) especially where there are no footpaths. Common prefixes are C/... for *Calle* & *Avda.* for Avenue. An **urban** residential road **without pedestrian paths** usually has a **20 kph** speed limit even if there are no signs stating as such.

- A *PASAJE* is a (foot) passage, and is not usually open to motor traffic.

- A *CARRETERA* is a **main trunk road** or a by-pass if through a town, **often 4-lanes** with a centre divider. It can be a national road. The limits are up to a posted **120 kph** (73 mph). A carretera may change into an *AUTOVIA* when leaving the city limits and will be signed as such. Prefix on a map is E, N or C.

- A *VIA RAPIDA* is a two-way, two lane (opposite directions) fast road. It will have junctions the same as any other road, but generally, unless otherwise posted, you have priority. The name is being phased out in 2004.

- An *AUTOVIA* is a "fast" dual four + lane carriageway (two each way) and is usually a national road. It may not be completely to motorway standards, Prefix is N, E or C.

- An *AUTOPISTA* is a motorway-classed road, which **can be a toll-road** *(PEAJE)*, built as a high-speed freeway / expressway. The limit for most vehicles is 120 kph, although you may see expensive cars doing expensive speeds (if they are caught). Toll rates are often **increased in summer** on the holiday routes. They are usually quite empty out of season as the Spanish, as elsewhere, do not like paying tolls. There is usually an alternative route.

Roads are signed by not only the national Spanish route number e. g. **N** or **A**, but also local and European route numbers: -

Road Prefix e.g. "N" followed by the number.	Type of road. Example signs are in part 7—1.
A	Autopista or Autovia.
	Via Rapida - These are being renamed in 2004, but the (green & white) signs may still be around for a while in some areas.
C	Carretera. Provincial main road. Often a dual carriageway, but not to motorway standards.
D	Destination or diversion (*desvio*) road. Not an autovia, etc.
E	European network number. Often continues into adjoining EU country.
N	National. A Spanish main trunk road. If followed by a Roman number (e.g. IV), the road is for the local Province only.

You may see more details on your (quality) Spanish road map.

Engine Horsepower.

The methods used in Spain for measuring engine power in Spain are *CV caballos de vapor* (or in French, *cheval-vap€*) and Kilowatts (Kw).   "**bhp**" (brake horse power) is the common UK and USA method of measurement, but the difference is very small between CV & bhp.

Kilowatts is the commonest modern international form of measurement.

100 cv = 98,632 bhp = 73,55 Kw.

Part 1-2
Glossary of Non-Technical Terms.

Spanish term	English Meaning	Notes
Abogado.	Lawyer or Solicitor.	The one you approach with a problem.
Asistencia en viajes.	Roadside assistance (breakdown on holiday, etc.).	Help by your insurance company, etc. who supplies you with the telephone number.
Automoviles Inspeccion Tecnica de Vehículos.	Listings are in the Yellow Pages for ITV test stations.	Where you take your vehicle for technical safety testing. (In UK— MOT).
Ayuntamiento	Town / city council.	
Baja de matrícula.	Vehicle scrapping certificate (accident or old age).	Mandatory to prevent the vehicle being rebuilt.
Bonificación.	No Claims Bonus	Insurance classification
Centros de Reconocimento Médico para Conductores.	Where you go for a medical for a Driving Licence.	Near the *Trafico* Offices, but usually a registered one in each town at a clinic.
Certificado de equivalencia.	Certificate (translation) issued by the RACE to accompany your foreign driving licence.	See Part 6—4 for more information.
Certificado Internacional de Seguro de Automóvil.	Known as "Green Card".	Extended cover for other EU countries. See note in Part 9 – 1.

Caballos de vapor (CV).	Horsepower (actual).	From the French calculation method.
Código de circulación.	Spanish Highway Code.	
Costa *or* Gasto de defensa.	Legal expense.	
Declaración jurada.	Sworn statement.	
Empadronamiento, Nota, *or* Certificado de Empadronamiento.	Electoral register, Noted on the… This is important to do as you need this form to obtain some documents such as a Spanish driving licence, to buy a new car in Spain, etc.	Often asked for as proof of residence in a your local area. Obtained at local town hall at usually **no cost**. Take your *escritura* or rental contract to obtain this simple document, as well as NIE/NIF and passport.
Franquicia.	Voluntary insurance excess.	You pay this first amount for any damage.
Garantía: Sin garantía.	Guarantee: Without guarantee	Sin = "without", e.g. *sin plomo*: unleaded petrol.
Gestor and gestoria	Business and legal advice agent and agency.	A legally qualified and registered advisor for all matters related to business and some legal, but not as highly qualified as a lawyer. Usually also a notary.
Homolgamación	Homolgamation.	An approved specification used to standardise vehicles (or signs) technically in the EU.

Limitado.	limited (cover?).	
Impuesto municipal sobre vehículos de tracción mecánica.	**Annual Road Tax**, paid at your local Town Hall (*Ayuntamiento*).	Must be usually before 20th May.
Impuesto sobre la circulación.	Vehicle registration tax.	On a new vehicle.
Impuesto Sobre Transmisiones Patrimoniales y Actos Jurídicos Documentados.	Transfer tax, 4% of the deemed value, by the authorities, of the vehicle.	Used when selling and buying a vehicle. The tax is usually paid by the buyer.
Incendio y robo.	Fire and theft, as in Third Party, Fire and Theft	
Inspección Tecnica de Vehíclos (ITV)	The vehicle roadworthy test procedure.	In Spain, any car over the mandatory periods (see Part 5-2) is subjected to a technical test at an **ITV** official test centre.
Jefatura provincial de trafico.	Provincial Traffic Office. Also called "El **Trafico**".	Where you may register a vehicle including change of ownership, obtain a driving licence, pay fines, etc.
Marca.	Car registration number.	
Matriculación.	Registration (of motor vehicle).	
Multa.	Traffic fine or penalty.	
Permisso de circulación.	Driving licence.	Also "*Carnet de Conducir*"
Potencia fiscal.	Fiscal horsepower.	Formula used to calculate road tax.

Precintado	Sealed.	Example, when Customs "seal" a motor vehicle for a period of time?
Real Automóvil Club de España. (RACE). Say it "**rathay**".	Royal Automobile Club of Spain.	Equivalent of the RAC or AA, etc. in the UK.
Residencia	Residence permission. When you live in Spain for more than six months each year, ie you officially live in Spain, not your country of origin.	In this context, it means the card issued by the authorities to register you as a full-time Spanish resident. Must be renewed every 2 / 5 years.
Se alquila.	"For rent" - notice.	
Se vende.	"For sale" - notice.	
Segundo mano *or* usado	Secondhand.	
Seguro de ocupantes.	Driver and passenger insurance.	Optional cover for injury and time off work.
Seguro obligatorio.	Compulsory insurance cover.	Third party is the minimum.
Solicitud de Carnet del Permiso de Conducir.	Application for a Driving Licence to drive.	Form TASA 2,3 at the *Trafico* office.

English	Spanish	Notes
Tarjeta de inspección técnica de vehículos.	Card issued when you first have your vehicle road-worthied by the **ITV**.	You also get a stick-on certificate which is placed on the top right hand side of your windscreen with the date due for the next test. Different colour each visit / year.
Todo riesgo.	Comprehensive insurance (all risks).	
Vehículo De Ocasión	"Bargain vehicle" (on sale).	Usually seen in dealerships and adverts.
Vigilantes Jurados.	Security Guards.	Usually armed.

ENGLISH	SPANISH	Notes
Accident Report Form issued by Insurance Companies.	Declaración Amistosa de Accidente de Automóvil. Also know as the Decl. de **Siniestro de Automovil**…	Completed by both or more drivers after an accident and sent to the Insurance companies ASAP.
Annual Road Tax, usually paid at your local Town Hall (*Ayuntamiento*)	Impuesto municipal sobre vehículos de tracción mecánica.	
Bargain vehicle, or Chance to buy a bargain vehicle.	Vehículo De Ocasión	Usually seen in motor dealerships and adverts.
Lawyer	Abogado	

Business and legal advisory **agent** and **agency**.	Gestor and gestoria.	A legally qualified and registered advisor for all matters related to business, but not as highly qualified as a lawyer. Can also be a notary.
Card recording when you first have your vehicle technically tested (road-worthy) when it is four years old, etc.	Tarjeta de inspección técnica de vehículos.	You also get a sticky certificate which is placed on the top right hand side of your windscreen with the date due for the next test. Different colour each year.
Certificate (translation) issued by the RACE to accompany your foreign driving licence.	Certificado de equivalencia.	Should have done if you have no International Driving Licence.
Electorial register, Noted on the...	Empadronamiento, Nota, or Certificado de,	Form showing proof of residence in a local area. Take your *escritura* or rental contract to the town hall to obtain this free, simple, useful document.
Comprehensive insurance (all risks).	Todo riesgo.	
Compulsory insurance cover.	Seguro obligatorio.	Third party is the minimum.
Driver and passenger insurance.	Seguro de ocupantes.	Optional cover for injury and time off work.

Driving licence.	Permiso de conducción.	Also "*Carnet de Conducir*"
Driving Licence Application.	Solicitud de Carnet del Permiso de Conducir	Form TASA 2,3 at the *Trafico* office.
Electorial register, Noted on the,	Empadronamiento, Nota, or Certificado de,	Form showing proof of residence in a local area. Take your escritura or rental contract to the town hall to obtain this simple document.
Fire and Theft, as in Third Party, Fire and Theft.	Incendio y Robo.	
Fiscal horsepower.	Potencia fiscal.	Formula used to calculate road tax.
"For rent", - notice.	"Se alquila".	
"For sale", - notice	"Se vende".	
Guarantee: Without guarantee	Garantía: Sin garantía	
Homolgamation	Homolgamación	A specification used to standardise vehicles technically, and some road signs.
Horsepower (actual).	Caballos de vapor (CV).	Method of showing engine power. (bhp or Kw).

Was known as a "Green Card".	Certificado Internacional de Seguro de Automóvil.	Extended cover for other EU countries. See note in Part 9 – 1.
Lawyer or Solicitor.	Abogado.	
Legal expenses.	Defensa Penal.	
Listing in the Yellow Pages for **ITV** test stations.	**A**utomoviles Inspeccion **T**ecnica de **V**ehiculos	
Medical for a Driving Licence.	Centro de Reconocimento Médico para Conductores.	Usually near the *Trafico* Offices or in local town.
No Claims Bonus.	Bonificacíon.	
Registration (of motor vehicle)	Matriculación	
Provincial Traffic Office.	Jefatura Provincial de Trafico. ("El Trafico")	Where you may register a vehicle including change of ownership, obtain a driving licence, pay fines, etc.
Registration number (of motor vehicle)	Matriculación	
Registration tax.	Impuesto sobre la circulacion	

Residence Permit.	Residencia.	In this context, it means the card issued by the *policia nacional* to register you as a Spanish resident. Must be renewed every five years.
Roadside assistance (on holiday, etc.).	Asistencia en viajes.	Roadside help by your insurance company or RAC, etc. Emergency telephone number is supplied on a card for you wallet.
Royal Automobile Club of Spain.	Real Automóvil Club de España. RACE.	Equivalent of the RAC or AA in the UK.
Sealed.	Precintado.	When Customs seal a motor vehicle for a period of time.
Secondhand (vehicle).	Segundo mano.	
Security guards.	Vigilantes jurados.	
Spanish Highway Code.	Código de circulación.	
Sworn statement.	Declaración jurada.	
The roadworthy test procedure.	Inspección Tecnica de Vehíclos (ITV)	In Spain, any car over the mandatory period (see part 5-2), is subjected to a test at an official ITV test centre.
Town/city council.	Ayuntamiento.	

Traffic fine or penalty.	Multa.	
Transfer tax, 4% of the deemed value of the vehicle.	Impuesto Sobre Transmisiones Patrimoniales y Actos Jurídicos Documentados.	Used when selling and buying a vehicle. The tax is usually paid by the buyer.
Unlimited (cover).	Ilimitado.	
Vehicle scrapping certificate.	Baja de matrícula.	Mandatory to prevent the vehicle being rebuilt.
Vehicle transfer tax form (No. 620).	Compra-venta de vehículos usados entre particulares.	Used to pay tax (4% on current value of vehicle) on transfer of ownership. Cannot register change without this being paid. Obtained from the *Hacienda* tax office or a tobacconist (*tabac*) shop.
Voluntary insurance excess.	Franquicia.	You pay this first amount for damage.
Wheel clamps.	Cepos	Used to immobilise a vehicle for parking in an illegal area.

Part 2-1

SURVIVING THE N340 CARRETERA / AUTOVIA.

The **N340** coast road on the Costa del Sol is often described as **the most dangerous road** in Spain (even Europe) and I have seen many shunt-type accidents where the several cars hit the ones in front, causing backups of several kilometres, proving that keeping the **2-second distance rule** (or more in the wet) from the vehicle in front, **is vital** on this road. In **medium to heavy traffic**, stay in the fast lane at traffic speed (usually 100 kph) keeping 2 + seconds from the vehicle in front. This allows vehicles to get on and off the N340 safely in the right hand lane and for you to avoid a "rear-ender". Ignore the few bad drivers who "bully" you to get past, unless of course there is no vehicle at all in front of you. The toll roads are generally very much safer, the few accidents on these roads being due to high-speed tyre failures (tyres too soft?) or poor driving skills.

MAPS AND ROADS.

Please note that we have **not included any Maps** in this book. Spain's roads have been improved dramatically in the last 10 to 15 years due to tourism needs and large grants of cash from the EU, which means that some of your taxes paid in your country have helped to improve the roads you drive on in Spain. New toll roads are still being built, and these greatly speed the travel times between main centres. Tolls generally are increased in the tourist holiday months (doubled, if you are a pessimist, and if an optimist, they are halved in winter months), and many Spanish drivers still use the older un-tolled roads **all year**, which are consequently crowded especially in the holiday months at the coast, and especially on the Costa Del Sol.

Good road maps (*mapas de carreteras*) are available at all garages and book-shops. The **RACE** (Royal Auto-Club of Spain) map book is especially useful.

Part 2-2

IMPORTANT GENERAL ADVICE.

If you are on holiday in Spain, or are using the roads here for the first time, the following advice is worth reading and following closely. At the most, it can save your life, and in the least, save you time and money.

Pedestrians from countries where they drive on the left.

You are used to **looking right for traffic** when crossing the road. There is usually one visitor from the UK killed every year and serious injuries where pedestrians step into the road after **looking the wrong way.** The golden rule I use is to **LOOK BOTH WAYS TWICE**, even when driving a car or motorcycle. Always make it an automatic action.

PLEASE MAKE IT A GOOD HABIT, ESPECIALLY FOR CHILDREN.

<u>Pedestrian Crossings</u>. Drivers are supposed to stop for pedestrians on these crossings painted with black and white blocks, but often **do not** in the big cities. Do not treat them as the UK "Zebra Crossings" where the pedestrian is "always in the right" after an accident. There is more information on crossings in **Part 6—2**. The Spanish highway code states that, as you **step onto the crossing, clearly show approaching drivers the palm of your raised hand** so they know you are going to cross the road. Still wait to see if they are going to stop though. Drivers do not have to assume that you wish to cross if you just stand on the pavement near the crossing.

Drivers/Riders

Beware of other people indicating to you that there is something wrong with your vehicle. Sometimes, this is a ploy to steal from your car. Always ensure that there is someone in the car to protect your goods if you stop to check e.g. a suspect tyre, with these people around. (I know that, like other such comments, this is repeated elsewhere in this book, but it is **so important**). Sometimes, robbers will cut your tyres and then offer to help, and then rob you when you take out your spare tyre (and your luggage) knowing that you cannot chase them. If you are on your own, lock your doors with the windows up. A minor bump from behind can mean a robbery attempt so be aware. A stolen handbag with travellers cheques, cash and other valuable documents is a major loss for you.

At a **service station**, when filled up with fuel and ready to pay, **if on your own**, do not leave the **car keys in the ignition, and lock the doors**. There are gangs of car thieves who steal a substantial number of cars or valuables from visitors to Spain when they go to pay for their fuel purchase. If you have a rental car, some criminals **follow you from the airport** and rob you at the first fuel stop, as they know that your fuel tank is probably empty and you will need to fill up.

It is against the Law to use a mobile phone in a service station as it may upset the radio links from the pumps to the cash desk.

While walking in the streets of crowded towns, especially holiday areas, ensure your documents and cash / travellers cheques are very secure. Scooter rider teams may even cut your handbag's strap, grab it and escape quickly. Use a handbag with a metal chain type strap to discourage them and wear it across your body. This especially applies if you are a senior citizen as you are an easy target to them. Remember you are going home soon and will not be there to identify suspected thieves subsequently arrested by the *policia locale* although a new **24-hour fast-justice Court system** is being introduced soon.

DO NOT BE A VICTIM.

TAP WATER QUALITY—ANDALUCIA.

In Spain, when you go into the service stations, car accessory shops or some supermarkets, you will see five-litre bottles of ready mixed coolant for sale in the motoring section. (You will also see much bottled drinking water sold in southern Spain).

Previously, the author who had lived in South Africa for 25 years where the tap water was very good, would buy the concentrate coolant and mix it with tap water, but especially in southern Spain you **should not** do this as there is (in Andalucia, at least) a high proportion of **corrosive** minerals in the tap water. While this is OK for drinking (it tastes OK), it corrodes the coolant systems in the cars and bikes over a relatively short period of time, so either use the ready-mix which has been made with **distilled water**, or make up your own using distilled water, which is also cheap and easy to find in the supermarkets, and the coolant concentrates.

On arrival in Spain, the author bought a four year-old Fiat Punto from a small car rental company where it had been regularly topped up with tap water by a well-meaning assistant, who obviously thought that the half-full coolant header tank was meant to be full.

In the first year of ownership, I had problems with a steel coolant system pipe rusting badly **on the inside** and eventually leaking through a rust pinhole (under pressure) on the *autopista*. It never happens near home. It cost much cash to rectify the overheated engine, so check the coolant when checking a prospective second-hand car purchase by taking a sample. If it is not a ready-mix liquid, identified usually by the orange or red colour, it is probably a good idea to look elsewhere for your new purchase.

If you are not mechanically minded, have the car checked by the technical section of the **RACE** (Royal Auto Club of Spain) or a competent workshop before paying over the cash.

USEFUL PHONE NUMBERS.

PLEASE NOTE THAT THE NEW (from 2002) EMERGENCY NUMBER IS 112

This is the equivalent of 999 in the UK, and 911 in the USA.

Please note that at these numbers, there is usually someone who speaks English.

Guardia Civil (national force: on the roads).	062
Municipal / local police, give your location.	092
Policia Nacional (National Police).	091
Comisaría de Policia, Malaga (town local police station)	952 04 62 00
Consulate, British, Alicante	965 21 69 22
Consulate, British, Malaga	952 3523 00
Consulate, Canada, in Malaga City	952 22 33 46
Consulate, Ireland, Fuengirola, Malaga	952 47 51 08
Consulate, USA, Fuengirola	952 47 48 91
Embassy, British, Madrid	913 08 52 01
Embassy, South Africa (Madrid only)	91 436 37 80

PART 3-1

DRIVING – SPEEDING PENALTIES

Generally, **except in urban areas**, the police in Spain allow speeds in excess of the posted speeds by **as much as 20%** without penalty, to allow for errors in speedometers, etc. (How sensible). It is hoped that the change recently reported in the UK Press will not be applied here, where after applying to the EU, a UK speeder trying to have his penalty quashed merely brought about a change in the Law that the exact speed recorded by the measuring device must be used in the charge, thus removing any leeway. Speeds in excess of 50% of the limit will result in licence suspension, a jail sentence, community service, compulsory attendance a traffic schools, and / or points penalties against your driving licence. The speed limit figures in the table are sign posted on the road in a red-bordered circle, with black lettering on a white background, or if at a road works, a similar yellow background sign. If you are a foreigner with no local fixed address (not registered in Spain), you may have your licence taken away by the police officer who stops you for speeding at twice the limit (or if drunk or on drugs, etc), and if you cannot pay bail, they may supply you with Spartan accommodation until you appear in Court.

The obvious advice is **do not speed**, especially in urban areas and especially if you are unfamiliar with driving on the right-hand side of the road. Being human you may find yourself driving over the limit occasionally. You may check the accuracy of your speedometer using the kilometre signs posted on most *autopistas* and *autovias* and by using a stop-watch and driving at a steady speed, recording the number of seconds between these posts. This will give you by calculation (see table in Part 3—2) a good indication of the accuracy of your car's speedometer.

Most cars over-read, for example, car speedometer reading 120 kph: actual timed speed may be 115 kph.

Always check our Web-site for new Laws and updates.

If stopped by the police, usually the *Guardia Civil* on the open road, and the *Policia Locale* in towns, be polite and patient. On the Costa del Sol, some of the police speak a little English, but generally, you may need your Spanish phrase book. Remember, Spanish Law dictates that you are **not allowed to have a radar speed-checking detecting device** in the car, and the police carry breathalysers to check for alcohol and are expected to soon to have easy-to-use drug testing equipment. (It has been broadcast that **one third** of accidents in Spain involve alcohol affected drivers). Make sure that you have all driving and car documents ready, and also the mandatory approved **reflective triangles and jackets,** and spare **light bulbs**. All can be bought as kits from car accessory shops and the larger supermarkets. If you wear **spectacles**, you may be asked to produce a **spare pair**. A new Law effective January 2004 states that drivers must carry an **approved reflective waistcoat** (*chaleco reflectante)* to use **at night and during the day,** if necessary, as a number of drivers changing wheels have been hit by other vehicles and killed or seriously injured. It must be kept inside the passenger section of the car, and be seen (by the police) from outside the car.

If given a spot fine, it must be paid in cash, and if you do not have cash, **as a visitor to Spain with no assets here**, you will be escorted to the nearest cash dispensing machine or Bank. If you have provable fixed assets here in Spain, or proof of living here for a year or more (a *residencia* card), you will be allowed to pay later as described in **Part 5 – 3**. The alternative is usually your car being impounded until the fine is paid. If you have exceeded the above maximum speed limits by 50%, including the driving licence suspension penalty limits, you may be arrested and appear in Court. The best alternative though is not to speed, especially in urban areas where your driving on the right-hand side of the road, places you at a disadvantage if you are used to driving on the left, especially when an emergency occurs and you react incorrectly.

Recently announced in the Press, certain local authorities (Tarifa is one) are engaging the services of a UK company to ensure collection of fines issued to UK tourists who leave without paying, usually parking fines where the police cannot wait by the car to collect them.

RADAR SPEED WARNING DEVICES.

It is forbidden in Spain to use these devices and if a driver is caught, regardless of the country of registration of the vehicle, a stiff fine will be levied. So if you have one fitted, disconnect it and hide it away.

To be fair, I have not been stopped in over four years, in fact I have not even seen a speed trap on the coasts, even during one fast June trip to Madrid and back in two days. They have been seen in Malaga city. Unlike the UK, where speed-trapping has become a profitable pastime for the police, the Spanish police have better things to do, especially stopping the drug-trafficking from North Africa. However, the much lower accident rates in the UK compared with Spain, prove that the UK is already doing something correctly as far as road safety is concerned.

Speed limits for car and motorcycles, from January 2004.

Types of Road > Vehicles.	Autovias & Autopistas	Carreteras and main country roads, as signed.	Roads outside of urban areas.
Cars and motorcycles.	120 kph (74 mph)	100 kph (62 mph)	90 kph (56 mph)
Vehicles derived from touring vehicles, eg Minibuses & autobuses.	100 kph	90 kph	80 kph (55 mph)
Trucks and vans over 3.500 kg, autocaravans and vehicles with a trailer of not more than 750 kg	90 kph	80 kph	70 kph (44 mph)
Cars with a trailer weighing more than 750 kg (1 650 lbs).	80 kph	80 kph	70 kph

PART 3-2

CHECKING YOUR VEHICLE SPEEDOMETER
FOR ACCURACY USING A STOP WATCH.

By dividing 3 600 seconds by the speed being checked over one kilometre, you will see whether or not your speedometer is accurate. Most speedometers are not accurate at higher speeds and generally over-read: that is they read that you are going faster than you actually are. This means that you can exceed the speed limit according to your speedometer by about 5% depending on your vehicle, without actually breaking the Law, but if you want to be sure, you can easily check your speed using the **kilometre sign-posts** on most *autopistas/autovias*. For find the equivalent mph, multiply the kilometre speed by 0,61 or use the conversion table in **Part 3—3.**

EXAMPLE

Speed being checked with stopwatch between kilometre signs = 100 kph. Drive your vehicle to set your speedo-reading to a constant indicated 100 kph (or 62 mph). In this example, the actual watch reading is 37,5 seconds.

3.600 / 37,5 = <u>96 kph</u>. **The true speed is 96 kph.**

EXAMPLE TIMINGS over One Kilometre.

True Speed, kph	Secs/Km	True Speed, kph	Secs/Km
35	103	80	45
50	72	90	40
60	60	100	36
70	51,5	120	30

For safety's sake, always do this check on an "empty" road.

To check KPH speeds if you only have an MPH Speedometer, refer to next page, Part 3—3 for conversion tables.

PART 3-3 , SPEED CONVERSION TABLES.

To convert **kph to mph** or **mph to kph**, select speed in mph or kph (**X**) in centre columns, and read in next column for converted speed.

MPH	X	KPH		MPH	X	KPH
18,6	30	48,3		86,9	140	225,3
21,7	35	56,3		90,0	145	233,3
24,8	40	64,4		93,2	150	241,4
21,7	35	56,3		96,3	155	249,4
31,1	50	80,5		99,4	160	257,4
34,2	55	88,5		102,5	165	265,5
37,3	60	96,5		105,6	170	273,5
40,4	65	104,6		108,7	175	281,6
43,5	70	112,6		111,8	180	289,6
46,6	75	120,7		114,9	185	297,7
49,7	80	128,7		118,0	190	305,7
52,8	85	136,8		121,1	195	313,8
55,9	90	144,8		124,2	200	321,8
59,0	95	152,9		130,4	210	337,9
62,1	100	160,9		133,5	215	345,9
65,2	105	168,9		136,6	220	354,0
68,3	110	177,0		139,7	225	362,0
71,4	115	185,0		142,8	230	370,1
74,5	120	193,1		145,9	235	378,1
77,6	125	201,1		149,0	240	386,2
80,7	130	209,2		152,1	245	394,2
83,8	135	217,2		155,3	250	402,3

Part 3—4.

BUYING FUEL IN SPAIN.

One of the first benefits that the British visitor will find is that fuel is much cheaper in Spain than in the UK, especially the difference in cost between petrol and diesel, and that is one reason why diesel cars are so popular in Spain. Over 50% of new cars sold each year in Spain are now diesel powered.

The following are a few notes of interest about buying fuel in Spain at the service stations (*gasolineras*).

There are now six motor fuels in Spain, and each supplier has their own brand name for them: -

⇒ **95 octane unleaded** (*sin plomo*), commonest used in modern cars.

⇒ **Super 98 octane unleaded**, for high performance cars.

⇒ **Diesel** (*gasoleo*), standard quality fuel for all diesel cars, turbo and non-turbo engines.

⇒ **Diesel** (BP Ultimate?). Higher quality for a few cents more per litre, but benefits have yet to be proved by long termindependent tests.

⇒ **97 octane Super** with a **lead replacement** chemical for older cars.

⇒ **Diesel**, cheap lower quality fuel for older engines. Much cheaper than normal diesel, about half price and was the only diesel fuel sold about 8 years ago. Very difficult to find now as very few service stations stock it.

It is necessary to ensure that you use the **correct fuel** for your car if it is a rental (assuming you are familiar with your own car). Most rental cars have the fuel needed on a sticker next to the filler cap. The hoses have colour codes and different nozzles for petrol and diesel as in the UK.

In Spain, as in most of Europe, in most service stations, you are expected to fill your tank yourself, and then go to a cash desk to pay. A receipt will be given if asked for - (*Recibo, por favor*—say it as "rethibo, por fabor"). Unless you have **adult and fit** passengers left in the car, *do not leave the keys* in the car or **even the doors unlocked**, while you pay, as it is not unknown for thieves to steal the car or its contents. While on the subject, beware of anyone trying to distract your attention **at any time** with for example, telling you that your tyre is flat. It could be a trick for an accomplice to steal from your car and they have been known to also cut your tyre so it will go flat. While you are taking your luggage out to get the spare tyre, they steal it and drive off. (I know that it has been written elsewhere in this book, but the author knows of someone who has been **"caught" twice**).

Due to some drivers filling up and speeding off without paying, some stations need you to pay say €.50 before they will let you fill-up. So if the pump does not work, this is often the reason. There will be a notice at the pump, but it is usually in Spanish (of course!).

You are not allowed to use your mobile phone, or any similar radio emitting device, while filling up. This is effective from January 2004.

Diesel fuel is about 17—20% cheaper than 95 unleaded, and when the extra economy of the modern turbo-diesel engine-car is considered, the overall added fuel economy in running a diesel in Spain can be as much as 40% with little usable difference in normal on-road performance. As in other countries, many garages have a shop at which you may buy newspapers, wines (yes, they sell alcohol as the Spanish are, in the main, considered to be adults once they reach 18 years of age, although the drink / drive limits are much lower than in the UK), bread, and other food; some have hot meals and drinks. Many also have car washes, either drive through, or with a three stage (soap, wax and wash) hand-held high-flow gun in a special bay. Also there are vacuum cleaners, water and air points.

In many Provinces in Spain especially Andalucia, it is illegal to wash your vehicle in the street (to save water and for safety reasons in the narrow streets), so these services at service stations or special wash-bays (e.g. Blue Elephant or *Elefante Azul*) are very useful, quick and cheap to use, and the water is re-used after filtering. They also have the benefit, or should have, of having **demineralised water** for the final wash, as the tap water in some Provinces, especially Andalucia, is very "limey" and can leave streaks on the bodywork if not immediately wiped clean.

PART 4-1

MORE GENERAL NOTES ON DRIVING IN SPAIN.

Some of the following also apply "at home", but should be emphasised due to the importance of observance in Spain to avoid spoiling your holiday, or worse.

⇒ **Road-junctions,** remember to give way to vehicles coming from **your left** (you may be used to right) if you are on the minor road. The **only time** you give way to traffic coming **from your right** is when road-sign markings dictate, and this can be, for example, on a roundabout or a "blind" T-junction. See **Part 7-1** for pictures of the road signs. The other common road sign is a **give way,** *ceda el paso* (white background, inverted triangular sign with a red border). Also there may (should be, if not worn away or covered in tyre wear and oil in the summer months) a give-way sign, an inverted white triangle, painted **ON** the road.

⇒ **Priority roads.** These are main roads and are marked with a yellow diamond on a white background for the priority traffic to follow, with a black diagonal line through the diamond when the priority ends. You have right of way.

⇒ **Emergency vehicles:** all have priority, including virtually anything with a siren or bell. Safely pull over and stop or visibly slow down so the driver knows he/she can safely pass. It is an offence (and silly) not to not do so.

⇒ **Wearing of seat belts,** if fitted, by **all persons** in the car, is mandatory in Spain, and the **driver can be fined** for anyone in the car not obeying this Law. Being caught without a seat belt, even in the rear seats, can cost you €.90 plus penalty points.

⇒ It is illegal to have a child aged **under twelve** in the front seats. Also, you may not have a child seat in the front due to possible injury from airbag inflation. Also, if in an accident where personal injury occurs, the insurance company concerned may refuse, or attempt to, in part or in full, to compensate the injured offender.

⇒ **Headlamps** must be used when driving after dusk/dark or in poor visibility, and this includes when other vehicle drivers may have problems in **seeing you,** and while the reader may think this point is the same everywhere, offenders abound and cause accidents. Places where headlamps should be on include tunnels (you are reminded before entering (*luces de cruz plus* a large rectangular sign of a dipped light), and after leaving, to switch them off. Make sure your headlamps are **converted** to driving on the right side of the road. See your car's handbook.

⇒ Flashing headlights behind a driver in the fast lane will cause him / her to move over into the right lane. Spanish drivers are usually very good at pulling over without this indication from the driver behind. Most offenders who stay in the outer lanes are usually foreigners or the younger, "macho" *señors* from major Spanish cities.

⇒ **Toll roads**. When approaching a set of payment booths, slow down well in advance. Have the cash ready to save time. Note the booths with a green arrow light over the lane: these are open. Note the sign for toll roads on page 100.

⇒ **Traffic lights**. Spain has saved millions by only having traffic lights installed, in most cases, at the point where the driver has to stop: that is not on the other side of the junction as well. This would have placed the first driver in line in a difficult position as the driver cannot see the traffic lights without peering forward and up. To overcome this problem, there are **miniature red and green** lights on the post holding the main lights **at driver eye-level** and you can use these to check when you can go if you are at the front of the queue.

The sequences are: -

RED for STOP.

FLASHING AMBER. Warning of the junction. **If safe to, PROCEED SLOWLY.**

GREEN—GO, **if safe to do so.** Check for traffic light "hoppers from usually left".

AMBER after GREEN, **STOP** if you have not passed the stop line or keep going if by stopping quickly may cause an accident (rear-ender). Police may be watching at these points and usually have a partner down the road to stop you if you do not obey this safety rule. The fine at present for running a red light is up to €.600.

⇒ **Flashing red lights** on a post at the side of the road are used to warn of traffic lights or another hazard ahead, or you are entering/in a restricted speed area.

⇒ When driving in heavy traffic on a dual carriageway (*autopista, autovia, carretera,* etc.) the author practises looking well ahead of the car in front and if the traffic is stalled ahead, uses the **car's hazard lights** (from January 2004, this is a legal requirement) and an arm held vertically out side the window. This will help prevent the dreaded shunt from behind).

⇒ It is a very necessary habit to be aware of drivers following too closely in Spain, and the author's car has been badly rammed from behind by a "dozy" (foreign) driver on the *carretera* (by-pass) who was not looking ahead and seeing, and taking action to avoid, a road jam 200 metres ahead.

⇒ **Slow driving** is one of the five main causes of accidents in Spain according to reports in the Press. It is significant that many of the older Spanish drivers did not get a car until late in life due to Spain's economic position under Franco and in the thirty-odd years since, so many "rode a donkey" or only a moped for many years. They are therefore not used to driving at speeds that many foreigners have grown up with, — but do tend to live a long stress-free life.

⇒ **Horns**. You are NOT ALLOWED to sound your horn **at night** in town especially residential areas and a fine up to €.60 will be given to offenders. Horns must only be used **in an emergency**.

⇒ Do not drive in **bus-lanes** except in an emergency, which must be then proven.

⇒ **White lines**. A single or double white line in the middle of the road, usually accompanied by the requisite signs, means no overtaking and the fines are very heavy, with penalty points or licence suspension for offenders.

⇒ It is illegal to "**undertake**" on a multi-lane highway (*autopista*, etc.), but not illegal to flash or signal drivers who are holding you up unnecessarily. Do not practice "road rage" as in an argument with the police, you will lose and they are **allowed** to "restrain you" using force and will do if necessary. Forget about claiming for assault by a policeman unless you are injured by more than a "clipped ear". If you are not used to driving on the Continent, this problem should not apply to you, of course, as you will be extra careful due to being unfamiliar with the roads, especially driving on the right.

⇒ **Motor scooters and mopeds**. It would appear that at least 50% of moped and scooter riders are suicidal, ignore all road laws, especially red lights and Stop street signs, and their high accident rates tend to prove this perception. **Do not get upset with them** unless they actually hit your vehicle or put your life in danger. Many do have accidents and they can often be seen riding their only means of transport with a leg in plaster, and it is the opinion of the author who used to ride and race motorcycles for many years, as well as being an volunteer instructor, that the police and parents do not take enough action to help them save themselves, although the police do have occasional "blitzes".

As it is, driving school instruction is not easy for these youngsters, many of whom ride without crash helmets and other protective clothing. They say it is too hot, even in Winter. Insurance for two-wheeled vehicles in Spain is consequently very high, and there have been complaints in the motoring Press about it, but the author can see no solution without intensive training and more action by the police and the parent's. Always give scooter /moped riders a wide berth.

⇒ You must have a **nationality identification plate** of your country fitted to the rear of your foreign vehicle, although with the new EU plates with this feature on them, this applies more to older vehicles.

⇒ **Snow chains** are compulsory on some (mountain?) roads when necessary, and road signs advise these areas. It is an offence to **not** drive with them fitted if the road is posted and the conditions are such that it is necessary because you may get stuck and block the road, or worse. You may also use studded tyres on such roads.

⇒ Cars must not be **overloaded**, especially with heavy roof luggage, although the French drivers do not seem aware of this Law, mainly those who are travelling to/ from North Africa. High gusty winds can cause such vehicles to be very "exciting" to drive, and also forces them to travel at very low speeds holding up normal traffic.

⇒ **Pet animals** must **be restrained** in a vehicle and **not allowed to be free** to romp around in the passenger section. (This also applies to children).

⇒ **Anti-glare** equipment (heavily-tinted glass, blinds, etc.) must not be fitted to the rear windows of vehicles unless two wing mirrors are fitted.

⇒ **Reversing** into side roads to effect a turn and three-point turns is not allowed in city / village streets. U-turns (one sweep) may be made on wide main single-carriageway roads when safe to do so. **Remember to turn left**, the opposite way to the UK.

⇒ Beware of donkeys, sheep and goats on narrow country roads. Some minor roads are very narrow especially in mountainous areas, with hairpin bends and blind corners. You should use your horn here for safety's sake, and listen for any other driver doing the same from the other way. Keep well to the right side of the road.

⇒ It has been said before in this book, but bears repeating. You are **not allowed** to use a **mobile phone** without a proper hands-free kit fitted in the car. This also includes the use of music equipment (a Walkman?) while being in charge of the car (driver). You are not allowed to even pull over to answer the mobile phone unless you are **completely off** the public road, and this includes the hard-shoulder which is part of the road. This Law has just been promulgated (2003) due to the high accident rates, and will probably (rightly) apply to all the EU as well in the future.

⇒ Those of us who are "good drivers" (the author has over 36 years of blame-free insurance no claims, despite riding at high speeds on motorcycles and in fast cars, with no licence endorsements so I suppose that qualifies) abhors the stupid habit of driving and talking into a handheld phone. It is legal to use a proper **hands-free system** with separate speaker and microphone though, even though this really is also a dangerous distraction.

IT IS IMPORTANT TO NOTE that , **even in a rental car**, you are expected to carry: -

⇒ Two EU APPROVED RED TRIANGLES which are to be placed at the side of the road, plainly visible to traffic, if you are forced to stop for any reason on or just off the road on the hard-shoulder. One is to be within 10-20 meters (yards) of the vehicle, and the other up to 100 metres away, facing the oncoming traffic, or if a narrow road, one facing each way about 50 to 100 metres away. The spacing depends on the speed of the traffic on that road. Carry a torch to warn other traffic also if necessary. Many people have been killed or seriously injured in Spain while working on their car after a breakdown at the side of the road.

⇒ SPARE LAMPS OR BULBS for your headlights and rear lights. If you are stopped by the police and do not have spare lamps / bulbs, you may be fined, especially if you have a failed lamp. You should also have the tools to change them.

⇒ A **reflective jacket (day and night)** or vest *(chaleco)*, EU approved, for use while working on the vehicle or walking on the road after a breakdown, etc. anywhere outside of a lit town area, even in daylight.   Effective January 2004.   Must be able to be seen from out side the car.

⇒ If you wear **spectacles** for driving, you may be asked to show a spare pair if stopped by the police.   Drivers again have used as an excuse that an accident was caused because they had mislaid or broke their spectacles and "had to drive".

CHECK LIST FOR YOUR, OR THE RENTAL, VEHICLE.

◆ **Approved reflective triangles.**   **2**

◆ **Spare set of lamps (bulbs).**   **1 set**

◆ **Approved reflective jacket/vest.**   **1 (or more).**

◆ **Plus, your spare spectacles if worn.**   **1**

Road Deaths per 100.000 Inhabitants of EU Member States.
For Year 2001.

When you read such figures, although one unnecessary death is to be deplored, **UK drivers** can be justly proud that despite the high density of traffic on the UK roads, their accident rate is the **lowest in Europe**.

5,9	**UK**	11	Italy
6,6	Sweden	13,4	Austria
6,9	Netherlands	13,5	Luxembourg
8,4	Finland	13,7	Belgium
9,5	Germany	**14,6**	**Spain**
9,7	Denmark	20,2	Greece
11	**Ireland**	21	Portugal

Other Checks When Collecting a Rental Vehicle.

⇒ Check for the **insurance card** and *permiso de circulation,* and manufacturer's **operator's book** (or at least, the tyre pressure table) usually kept in the glove compartment. Ask the rental staff to show you them and do not be put off by their "being busy".

⇒ Check that you have a copy of the **Insurance Report Form** in your language— **ENGLISH**. This is important if you have an accident where the other driver does not speak English. A copy is in the back of this book.

⇒ Exterior **bodywork for damage**. Report **every mark** before signing for car.

⇒ **Wheel trims**, all there and secure. Most companies now remove them as they are stolen or fall off and you are then subsequently charged for replacing them.

⇒ **Engine oil and radiator levels**. Check these with the agent present. The author has collected cars with very low oil level, and you are charged for any engine damage caused.

⇒ Check exhaust is clear with engine running "hard": no **excessive blue or black smoke** from the exhaust.

⇒ **Tyre pressures, as soon as possible**. The author has rented cars in many parts of the world, and experience shows that, in as much as **80% of cases** the tyres are **under-inflated**, often dangerously so. As in any country, as the driver, **you are responsible** in the event of an accident. If you are not sure of the pressure, 200 kpa or 2 bars (32 psi) is safe unless you are heavily laden, then 220 to 240 kpa. (Again, be careful of thieves at the first service area).

SPECIAL NOTE FOR RENTAL CAR FINANCES.

Please remember that the rental company **has your credit card number** and may debit your card **after** you have returned and left the car. They are also under Spanish Law have to give your full details to the police in the event of an offence being committed while the car was in your "charge". Make sure that the fuel level in the tank is as taken. Some rental companies supply the car with a full tank and it must be returned as such, others, the tank can be empty when returned as it was when collected.

PART 4 – 2.

DRIVING A FOREIGN-PLATED VEHICLE IN SPAIN.

A. Foreigner—anyone who is not a citizen or permanent resident (has *residencia*) in Spain.

B. Foreign plated car—any vehicle not on Spanish registration plates.

As a tourist or visitor, you are **not** permitted to use your foreign passenger car or motorcycle in Spain for more than six months in any one **calendar year.** This can effectively be extended to a year if from July of one year to June of the next. Commercial (working) vehicles are restricted to a one month but must be driven out of Spain and back (on business?) to qualify and they must not be used locally for deliveries or business, only for delivering from / to outside Spain, etc. It is essential in all cases that the driver / owner can prove that he / she is obeying the Law, and is not up to the police to prove that you are not, and it has been known where the police, during a roadside check, have charged drivers (usually commercials) where the car is only **suspected** of being operated illegally.

For private vehicles and as an **EU citizen**, you are classified as a tourist if you stay less than six months in Spain. If you intend to stay for at least six months, you should register for an **NIE** (*numero de identificación de extranjero*, or foreigner's identification number). There is no charge for this and it is easy: you do it yourself (details in Part 11 –1). This makes it much easier to be identified by the authorities and anywhere else identification could be required without having to carry your passport, although, I also carry a photocopy of my passport and have had it accepted with no exceptions. Longer than six months, then you must register (*residencia):* a small charge is made for this to cover the cost of the card, which will fit into your wallet / purse, with your photo on it. Spain is then classified as your main place of residence and then you pay taxes here, etc. When you take out *residencia, if applicable,* you then have **one month** to re-register your car onto Spanish plates (unless you qualify as below) and then you must also obtain a **Spanish Driving Licence**. (See Part 6 – 4) You can keep your foreign licence, but the Spanish one is OK for use anywhere in the EU as long as the details in the chapter on Driving Licences, Part 6 – 4, are satisfied.   (Note that you may only be insured for 3 holiday months though).

The six-month vehicle usage rule period can be any period as long as the **total does not exceed six months** in **any calendar year**. If you holiday here or only spend **up to** six months of the year here, you may keep the vehicle on foreign plates indefinitely as long as it is **insured and roadworthy** (current annual inspection where applicable, from the country it is registered in), plus road taxes paid in the country of origin, but be careful that you can prove at the side of the road (police check) that you are not using it more than the six months. Obviously, you will living in Spain less than six months of each year to be able to do this. To satisfy the police at a road side stop, you may be able to have the technical inspection carried out at the Spanish ITV station, but do not expect it to be plain sailing unless you choose a station where they have done it often before, and it is suggested that you use a *gestor* specialising in this service.   Also, if you drive back to the UK (etc.), the vehicle must have the current UK-MOT certificate **as soon as you drive onto UK soil:** an impossibility in practice.

However, you should protect yourself from unnecessary Spanish police charges where they **suspect** that you are not obeying this Law. The police, especially the *Guardia Civil* are patrolling the main roads looking for drug dealers so they randomly stop vehicles, and they may choose you and if **you cannot prove** that you are **not resident** here (for less than six months per year, and consequently using the car within the six month rule), they will charge you and it is up to you to prove that you are innocent, even if you have been here only a month, remembering that, if you an EU citizen, your passport will not be stamped to prove this.   Carry copies of documents to prove this such as airplane, boat or train tickets, etc.   If you are caught and **proven to be resident** here, you may also be forced to register the car in Spain, with the taxes to pay, and **still be fined**, or have the car impounded, or at least have to employ a lawyer to sort out the problem.

While this may seem unfair, many foreigners use their cars for sometimes years without paying Spanish or their home country's taxes and, especially if it is an old vehicle, with it being un-roadworthy and a potential danger to all. Also, the insurance company will not usually pay out more than the minimum dictated by law if you have an accident and then claim it from you if you were not driving within the Law and their policy rules. The author has heard of people driving without insurance at all because they discovered that they could not get insurance locally, especially if the vehicle is over ten years old, and their company in the foreign country would probably not cover the risk if they knew that was being driven mainly or totally in Spain without their knowledge.

Spanish insurance companies (not an insurance broker who can do it through, for example, Gibraltar) generally will not insure a foreign car in Spain, although you may be able to do it through the Spanish Branch of a UK company (in Gibraltar?), remembering that a car that is not roadworthy (no annual inspection carried out') is generally not insured according to many of the insurance companies' rules. Study the policy small print.

It is not unknown for the police to note when a vehicle is being driven consistently for more than the six months (outside the local school is a favourite place), and to take action against you, and the author personally knows of "victims". You may apply to the local **Customs** officials (*aduanas*) for your vehicle to be "sealed" (*precintado*) and "unsealed" when you are not using it, so that you have proof that you are obeying the Law. The a*duana* will notify the local *Guardia Civil* who will actually carry out the sealing, which is usually merely placing a special "seal" tape usually across the steering wheel on a car, and the handlebars on a motorcycle. The process is not expensive but fines are quite heavy for those who are caught breaking these Laws. Also, make sure that you have a safe place to park the vehicle, certainly off the public roads. Apart from vandalism problems, the vehicle may be towed away and scrapped by the police as "*abandonado*" - abandoned.

YOUR FOREIGN PLATED VEHICLE.

If you take out *Residencia* (intend to live here as your main place of residence), then you have to put your owned foreign-plated vehicle onto Spanish plates **within one month** from when *residencia* is granted. Not many people know this but the officers of the *Guardia Civil* do, and the author has a copy of an actual *Guardia Civil* charge sheet with a stiff fine for this offence, issued to an English driver.

If you take up full residence in Spain, it is better to **buy a vehicle with Spanish registration** to use in Spain. You can have your vehicle transferred to Spanish plates.

However, due to the procedures, cost of transfer, resale price and the (minor) problem of a left-hand drive (steering wheel on the right) vehicle in Spain and the EU, unless the vehicle is a valuable classic, etc., **it is better to buy a Spanish-plated vehicle**.

IMPORTING A VEHICLE TO SPAIN FOR OFFICIAL RESIDENCE.

If you wish to import a vehicle into Spain as you intend to live here for more than the six months but **intend to return with it** to your own country, the following notes apply, but it is advised that for your specific need, you place it in the hands of a Spanish advisor (*gestor*) or lawyer (*abogado*) as they will know **the latest rules** as far as Spain is concerned, and how to smooth the paperwork through the system. Check with the local **Consulate for your country of origin or** where you wish to return to with the vehicle for the rules in that eventual destination.

EU CITIZENS.

Vehicles owned by the EU citizen & sales taxes paid in country of origin. The importation will be exempt from **import duties** and **registration taxes**, but not fees to carry out the registration procedure, plus the cost of using an advisor (*gestor*). The conditions are: -

⇒ You must have owned the vehicle for at least six months.

⇒ The procedure applies to caravans and trailers, but vehicles with engines of up to 49 cc are not classified for this purpose as a "motor vehicle" and may be imported as personal belongings.

⇒ It must have originated in an EU country (see below, homologation, non-EU citizens).

⇒ You must have paid VAT (*IVA*) or sales tax in the country of origin, and have proof of this. If not, then you will have to pay VAT at the 16% rate based on the local value of the vehicle as laid down in the tax authorities tables.)

⇒ You must obtain a **certificate of non-residence** (*baja de residencia*) for the period concerned from the country **you are leaving**. This certificate can be obtained usually from the local town hall of the country you are leaving, **OR** it can be a declaration made to the Spanish Consulate in the country you are leaving, **OR,** it can be made at your local Consulate (i. e., British if you are British) very soon (one month?) after you arrive here.

$\Rightarrow$ You must also be able to prove residence with your local property deeds (*nota simple*) or a current rental contract for at least one year.

The issued certificate may then be attached to your vehicle importation papers. It should be noted that these procedures must be started **within one month** of the issue of your Residence Permit issue date. I know, it is repeated in this book, but people who have lived here for years do not know this when questioned by myself. It is recommended that, if your Spanish language skill is weak, you should use an expert advisor (*gestor*) , as this is not a common procedure.

NON-EU CITIZENS.

The same rule applies as above, as far as using a vehicle without Spanish registration, that is, no more than six months in any one calendar year.   **As a Non-EU person**, if you are visiting here for any length of time, you may buy a vehicle and register it on **tourist plates (*matricula turista*)** if you intend to export it back to your original country at some time in the future. However, you must pay local road tax and it must comply with local Laws. This saves you paying Spanish VAT (or any EU) taxes other than the road tax, if it is intended to export it back to your own country if the regulations there allow it. You will need to clarify these details in your original country.   As far as buying the vehicle and registering it on a tourist plan, use a local main dealer **who is familiar** with the procedure, or a *gestor*, who will carry out the procedure for you.   It is not done very often.

PERMANENTLY IMPORTING VEHICLES OWNED BY A NON-EU CITIZEN.

The importation will be exempt from import duties and registration taxes, but not fees to carry out the registration and the costs if using an advisor (*gestor*). The conditions are: -
The vehicle must be standard to EU specifications for that vehicle, known as homologation (*homolgomación*). To ensure that it does, a certificate called a *ficha reducida,* must be issued by the manufacturer and this can be organised through the local main official dealership for the make of vehicle. It will cost from about €.140 to 500, depending on the size and type of vehicle (much less for motorcycles), and can take sometimes a couple of weeks or more to complete, and consists of the vehicle being inspected by the dealer who then organises the certificate from the manufacturer.

⇒ This applies to any motor vehicle imported into Spain whether it is **owned by an EU citizen** or not. That is, if it was not manufactured or previously licensed in the EU. So an owner bringing in a vehicle from a non-EU country will have to have it homologated (approved officially).

⇒ The procedure applies to caravans and trailers, but not to vehicles with engines of up to 49 cc.

⇒ You will have to pay VAT (IVA) based on 16% of the local value of the car depending on its age.

⇒ You must obtain a **certificate of non-residence** (*baja de residencia*) from the country you are leaving. This certificate can be obtained usually from the local town hall of the country you are leaving, **OR** it can be a declaration made to the Spanish Consulate in the country you are leaving, **OR,** it can be made at your local Consulate (i.e. British if you are British) **very soon** after you arrive here.

⇒ The vehicle will have to pass the local roadworthy test (IVT) and cannot be driven on Spanish roads until this has been done, and you will be issued with temporary plates to allow you to complete only this action during the application procedure, usually a week.

There is a lot involved, and it is recommended for the newcomer to Spain, that you place this work in the hands of a *gestor* who is not only legally qualified to offer these services, but is also up to date with any new changes in the Laws.

However, as I have written before, unless the vehicle is a "classic" or you really want to keep it here,

DO NOT BOTHER.

PART 5-1
THE POLICE FORCES IN SPAIN

There are basically three types of police (on the road) in Spain. They are: -

⇒ **National Police** (*Policía Nacional*).   This is the police force mainly concerned with serious crimes, and the detectives who investigate murder, etc., belong to the *Policia Nacional*. They have a police station, called a **comisaria**, in the larger towns, and like all policemen in Spain, they are armed.   If you are not officially employed in Spain, the foreigner's residence (residencia and NIE) registration is carried out at certain of these stations. Their uniforms are brown.

⇒ **Local Municipal Police** (*Policia Municipal* or *Policia Local*). These are employed by the local councils (*ayuntimientos*) and stay in that area for most of their lives or until they leave the job. They are responsible more for the minor problems in their area including local traffic control. They are recognised by their dark blue uniforms and black & white chequered hats.

⇒ *Guardia Civil.*   This force is national and specialises in country areas where there is no Policia Local, as well as the big towns on specific duties. This force patrols the national highways controlling traffic as well as all the other policing duties.   They often ride powerful motorcycles, in pairs on the main roads, have some mechanical knowledge and are trained in first aid. You will also see their (usually 4 x 4) vehicles on the highways, or driving along the beaches looking for drug-smugglers and illegal immigrants, or parked somewhere observing traffic. Many of the routes from Africa, used by drug smugglers and illegal immigrants to Europe, are through Spain.   They will assist you in an emergency, as well as carry out tests for driving under the influence of alcohol or drugs. The *Guardia Civil* live mainly in enclosed accommodation with their families, and so are protected from the personal threats of criminals.   They are dressed in green uniforms, and in "dress" uniform, wear the distinctive shiny hats. They are part of the military forces in Spain.

In the Basque country, in North– Western Spain, and in Catalonia, there are some other regional police forces as well.   As a point of interest, the languages spoken in these last two areas are of a different dialect to the Spanish heard in the rest of Spain.   Locals in Andalucia admit that they cannot easily understand these "foreign, —to them " dialects". And the Basques (of ETA terrorist infamy) have an almost totally different language again.

Other Notes.

⇒   The police use football referee type whistles a lot to get attention and give instruction. Be aware, especially in town at intersections. I carry one on my key ring to attract attention in town just in case someone "mugs" my wife and I.

⇒   While many UK visitors may be unused to seeing the police armed, the author, having lived in the USA and South Africa welcomes this aid to their (and our) protection, especially with the armed drug smugglers and organised crime (usually foreigners) in Spain.   Most murders in Spain are caused during shoot-outs by drug gangs, and by domestic problems.

⇒   Always be polite. The police, although in the author's experience have always been found to be very polite, are not unknown to literally administer a "clip to the ear" of those who give them violent or noisy problems, **especially younger people**. Forget about suing them for assault. You will be ignored.

⇒   The police often set up check points (*Control de Galibo*) for drinking and drug offences, or even just checking your car papers. You must always carry your car papers (**and your driving licence**), even if it is a rental car (they should be in the glove compartment). You may carry copies of these papers but they should be notarised by a Spanish *gestoria* , or at your local town hall (much cheaper) using their *"certificado"* stamp, as forgeries are not unknown.   You could be detained for not having these papers with you. Many town halls in the coastal holiday areas have a "Foreigner's Department", and they are most helpful with any advice, and they speak excellent English. To help with the certification of the car papers, we have found a small box of chocolates works wonders.

PART 5-2

EU VEHICLE TESTING.

This table shows, at this time, the safety inspection for roadworthiness testing standards for private vehicles throughout the EU. The test is known in the UK as the "MOT", or Ministry of Transport Test. The years are noted from the date of first registration. "Free" means no test needed in this period. The other countries are listed for your convenience, and more countries join in May 2004.

Austria.	Annually.
Belgium.	Annually from four free years after registration.
Denmark.	Four years free and then every two years.
Finland.	Annually from three free years.
France.	Every two years.
Germany.	Three free years, and then every two years.
Greece.	Every three years.
Ireland	Four free years, then every two years
Italy.	Four free years then every two years.
Luxembourg.	Three and a half years free than annually.
Netherlands	Three free years, then annually.
Portugal.	Four years free, then every two years.
Spain.	**Private cars**, four years free, then every two years until ten years old, then annually until scrapped. **Service vehicles**, (taxis and rental cars/bikes), two years free than every two years. **Motorcycles**. Free five years; then every two years until ten years old. **Commercial, up to 3.500 kg.** Every two years. free, then every year. **Over 3.500 kg**, every year.
Sweden.	Two free years, then two more years, then annually from 5th year.
Switzerland.	Four free years, then three years, and then every two years.
UK	Three free years, then annually.

Please note that as a visitor in your own car, your car does not have to conform to the Spanish testing standards, unless, of course, it is on Spanish plates.   It must, however, conform to the owner's/registering country's standards, including a current certificate of road-worthiness which must be carried in the car.

A question sometimes asked by residents who still have their cars on British registration plates is can I take my car to Gibraltar for the MOT?   The answer is NO, as only cars with GBZ (Gibraltar plates) are accepted by the Gibraltar testing authority.

Your car must be **taken back to the UK** for this test, or put on Spanish plates which at this time also means registering your foreign EU licence or obtaining a Spanish driving licence **depending on your residencial status**.

Repeated here as it is not generally known: **if you take out *residencia*, you must put your foreign plated car onto Spanish plates within 30 days.** *Residencia* means that you intend to live here as your main place of residence and that automatically means over six months per year.   The author has a copy of a charge sheet issued by the Guardia Civil for just this offence, committed by an English resident (name blanked out) here who did not take this action within the 30-days allowed and was caught in a road-block check.

Please do not forget that updates to this book are to be found on the web site at

www.spainvia.com/motoringinspain.htm

PART 5-3

Penalties, Traffic Fines (*Multas*).

As in any country, a system of fines is used to punish driver / riders / pedestrians who break the Law, and, as in any other country, ignorance of the Law is no excuse. Fortunately in Spain, it is not considered a necessary source of income for the authorities.

The Spanish police are very human, and especially in the tourist areas, tolerant of those visitors who may not be aware of minor local Laws, and will exercise discretion if the driver is polite when stopped, and if the misdemeanour causes no serious danger to other road users, unless the driver is drunk or using drugs, of course.

Fines, or *multas*, are set to discourage offenders from repeating offences and can spoil a visitor's holiday.   Offences are set as **minor (*leve*), serious (*grave*)**, and **very serious (*muy grave*)**.   The levels of fines are soon to be reset, but to give some idea: minor offences can carry a fine up to €.100 (£56), serious up to €.300 (£186) and very serious, €.1.500 plus (£930+), with possible licence suspension and/or penalty points.

A new Law in Spain is that you can now be fined for **following the vehicle in front too closely**, the fines being between €.90 to €.600.   As our BMW was smashed in 2001 from the rear by a Mercedes driver (we crash only with the most expensive) two years ago, I agree with this Law.   The driver was Ukrainian and could not speak Spanish or English which caused a problem, but luckily no one was hurt. We were insured with the same company so that made claiming easier – on his insurance, thus retaining my thirty-six years of no claims bonuses.

As a visitor, if you cannot pay on the spot or **have no assets** in Spain, you will be escorted to a cash point or bank to withdraw the **cash** (no cheques, etc.) and if you are unable to do this, you may have your vehicle impounded until the fine is paid.

If you pay **on the spot**, a 30% discount usually applies and also applies if paid within ten days.

If you have property in Spain, then you can be issued with a summons called a *boletin de denuncia*, and you can pay when you get home.   The fine must be paid within 30 days. You may pay the fine at any post office (*correos*) using a P.O. money order (*giro postal*) or at the *Trafico* office.

ALWAYS MAKE SURE YOU GET A RECEIPT FOR PAYMENT.

DRINKING AND DRIVING IN SPAIN.

I am of the opinion that drinking substantial amounts of alcohol up to 12 hours before driving, especially where the amount is so high that the driver is still drunk the next morning should be totally banned.   However, this is impractical to enforce so the only practical solution is to **condition people's minds** that it is very anti-social to drive drunk, or under the influence of any mind-altering drugs.   That is, the driver of the vehicle should not even be served with alcohol.   If caught, the vehicle should be confiscated — for good.

Readers may be perhaps annoyed or shocked to read that statement: perhaps many will agree, especially those who have lost a loved one due to the actions of a drunken driver. As a volunteer police reservist in years gone by, I have, on eight occasions, had to wake up in the early hours of the morning, parents, wives or relatives to tell them that their loved one / s was killed in a road accident the night before.   I have made too many cups of coffee in strange kitchens while these relatives are crying in the lounge, and sometimes on my shoulder.   In all cases, the accident victims reeked of alcohol.   On top of these, there were many more where there were serious injuries for the same reason.

It is only by admitting to these unnecessary tragedies that I feel justified in making that statement.   In the days of my youth, I have also had friends killed or seriously maimed by drunken car drivers subsequently fined a trifling amount for being drunk in charge of a motor vehicle. My friends were mainly on motorcycles and had drunk only coffee.

In Spain, the maximum allowed is 0,5 grammes per litre of breathed air (breathalyser), which is **much lower** than in other European Union countries, especially the UK.   Still, far too may Spaniards (and visitors) die each year due to drunken, or drugged, drivers.   It is worth noting that in the **first two years** following the issue of the driving licence, the maximum is 0,15 mg per litre of blood, and subsequently, 0,25 ml per litre and pedal-cyclists are also liable for penalties if caught drunk on the roads.. For public service drivers (buses and taxis, etc) and commercial vehicles (trucks, etc) the limits are far lower.

It is really no secret. The best thing is not to drink and drive. If you are caught, you will be asked to take a test (for alcohol or drugs), and **refusal** will result in a charge of **civil disobedience**, which often carries a harsher penalty than being over the limit.

The penalties effective from January 2004, now include up to six months in jail, stiff fines and community service. You can have your licence taken by the police officer on the spot (failing the breathalyser/drug test machine) as a precaution so you may not drive until the case is settled. You will also be arrested and spend at least one night in jail, and your country's relevant driving licencing office may be advised of the offence so the sentence can be also "in force" at home.

PLEASE BE WARNED.

As already stated, the **Criminal Courts** in Spain can, and often do, **award sometimes substantial damages** to the plaintiff, especially in the event of a motor accident. If you are the guilty party, your insurance will cover a certain amount, but anything over this, you are liable to pay out of your assets. An example would be where a driver does not insist on a passenger (the driver's family members are not covered by the driver's third-party injury insurance) wearing a seat belt, or the driver is drunk, or his / her car has faulty tyres. This is because the injuries would have been deemed to have been far less serious if the person/s had been wearing the seat belt/s, not drunk, bad tyres, etc.

PART 5—4
NEW LAWS FROM JANUARY 2004.

- **Alcohol and drugs**, driving under the influence. Greater penalties include, a jail sentence of three to six months, and/or a fine, and / or community service for 31 to 90 days, and licence confiscation for up to a year. The police may keep the driver's licence at the scene of the offence.

- **Driver education.** The government is proposing that regional authorities are to include road safety as a subject for school students from 12 to 16 years of age. When they pass, a certificate will be issued..

- **Motorcycles** must pass the ITV (MOT?) mechanical safety test.

- **New drivers.** Any driver who commits three serious or two very serious offences in two years, he / she will have the licence revoked and be unable to have another for at least one year, and must attend retraining courses before being reinstated.

- **Moped licences.** Holders who commit two serious offences, or one very serious offence in a two year period, will have their licence revoked.

- **EU Approved Safety-jackets.** These are now compulsory and must be worn outside the vehicle in during a break-down or an emergency situation at any time outside of a residential area (not just in poor visibility). These are usually used when your vehicle has broken down. At present, you are expected to carry one in the car / moto and many sensible moto-riders have one as part of their riding clothes for normal riding. They must be kept inside the people section of the vehicle, so they can be put on before getting out, and visible from outside the car.

- **Re-education courses.** Local authorities are to implement the availablity of these courses for offenders to attend as instructed by the Courts.

- **Re-offenders.** A driver will be considered a re-offender with three serious offences in a period of two years, and can be heavily fined with loss of licence. The loss can be avoided if the three are committed in more than one year (the minimum period) and if the offender agrees **and** satisfactorily attends the specified re-education courses.

- **Driving without insurance.** At the moment, this is a jailable offence. It is proposed to re-classify this so that instead, the vehicle will be confiscated until proof of insurance is shown, and a heavy fine is paid.

- **Children up to the age of three** must be seated and strapped in an approved child's car-seat in the **rear seats** of the car, as many cars now have front airbags that can injure a baby. Children over this age and under 150 cm (approx. 4 ft 9 ins.) must wear an approved seat belt that fits correctly. Under 13 year-olds, are not allowed to sit in the front seats.

- The use of **video, DVD or Internet screens by the driver** is forbidden in the car while it is on the highway . Drivers must leave the road completely to use these devices so the car will not be stopped causing a hazard to others. Excepted are special screens used to give rear views instead of wing mirrors, as on some new cars, or car reversing systems.

- **Mobile phones.** Only true hands-free phones, where the speaker is **not** attached to the driver's ear / s, are allowed. The author has already knowledge of fines of €.300 for this offence being issued.

- **Cyclists** may ride closely, two abreast on the right hand side of the highways as long as they do not cause a hazard to other road-users. They must wear approved safety helmets outside of urban areas.

- Heavy penalties for drivers who have a **radar speed checking device** to warn of such official speed traps. This includes all foreign cars.

While many may be annoyed at the plethora of new Laws, most are for good reasons, mainly based on actual accidents. Spain has one of the highest death rates on the roads in the EU, and in 2002, 433 pedestrians were killed on the roads. Officially conducted polls show that about 60% of children are not strapped into the car's seat, and those under three, or 150 cm, of course, are not big enough to use the normal seat belts.

The Police Forces, especially the *Guardia Civil,* have been motivated to apply these and existing road safety laws, to reduce the high death and injury rates in Spain, so please be warned and be aware. **New 2004 road signs are on pages 98 –101.**

PART 6-1

DRIVING IN THE SPANISH TOWNS/CITIES.

The advice here applies to most cities, towns and villages.

All the major cities are beautiful, especially in the old centres, many of which are restored or being restored as traffic free tourist areas. The buildings and old palaces (*palacios)* are well worth visiting and many tourists miss a lot by sticking to the beaches and the bars while on holiday. The rental car business in Spain is very competitive, and in summer, always book well ahead. Make sure it is air-conditioned in the summer: from December to May, you do not need air-conditioning in the car. There are no charges for mileage.

The author's advice on driving in **Madrid** is, if possible, **don't!** The traffic is very dense, the streets often narrow, especially the older back-streets, and parking almost impossible. The best way to see Madrid is by underground (*metro*), taxi, bus, or organised tour. **Barcelona** and other cities all suffer from the same problem to a lesser degree.

Malaga City, in the Province of Malaga is on the south coast on the Costa Del Sol, was not really a tourist city due to the bulk of the suitably prepared destinations being along the coast from Nerja to Gibraltar. However it is now worth a visit if you appreciate some of the attractions such as the recently opened Picasso Museum, the cathedral and Gilbofaro.

There are some points to note with driving in **Malaga**, as in many other older Spanish cities. These are (to name a few): -

Road name plates in the cities, especially Malaga, may be a series of pretty but impractical ceramic plates placed high on a building where, unless you have a pair of binoculars, you cannot easily read them. They are also few in number, possibly only one at a complex intersection, or only on one side of the road.

Direct left turns are often forbidden to keep the traffic flowing, but watch out for a road junction where a large roundabout is built into it. To turn left or go back the way you have just come, you turn right, **follow the road around the roundabout** (keep on the circumference, do not turn back into the main carriageway) and you should be driving back the way you came without stopping, unless you are late in turning and catch the traffic lights.

This forbidding of making direct left turns applies on many two-way roads as well, and they are well sign-posted. Refer to Page 90 for details. Usually you only have a short distance to go to reach a roundabout or junction where turning is easy without causing a traffic-jam or accident, but if you cheat and disobey the sign, you may hear the piercing sound of a policeman's football whistle, and then be involved in a discussion on your misdemeanour, with the usual paperwork, possibly getting a "red-card *(multa)*" .

Rear view mirror advice.

It is a good idea when parking in the **narrow streets**, to fold your door / wing mirror back on the traffic side **and** on the path side if it is very narrow, as it is not uncommon to see these mirrors hanging down after they have been hit by a truck or another car, --- or a disgruntled pedestrian whose passage on a narrow path was blocked.

TYRE TREAD DEPTH.

It is unusual now to see a vehicle with tyres that are worn beyond the point of minimum safety as far as tread-depth is concerned. The minimum depth for tyres in Spain on cars and motos is **1,5 mm** (1/16th of an inch). Please remember that if you have an accident while driving a vehicle with tyres below this depth, you could end up with your insurance company refusing personal damage payout, an expensive action for you, especially if the other party suffers injuries.

With a tread depth of even 2 mm, in heavy rain, speeds have to be kept very low (not more than 90 kph—55 mph) to avoid sliding or aquaplaning in an emergency, even with ABS braking fitted to the car. Some drivers think that ABS braking means that their car will stop in a shorter distance, even in the wet. This is true, but you will still have to have adequate space to stop in.

PART 6-2

PEDESTRIAN'S RESPONSIBILITIES.

The chance of at least one UK pedestrian visitor per year in Spain being killed is high because he / she stepped into the road after **looking the wrong way.** Many more are injured. A recent report stated that **nearly 50%** of those killed in road accidents in the Province of Malaga, on the Costa del Sol in 2002, were **pedestrians**. The dreaded N340 coastal road (reputed to be the most dangerous road in Spain) has camping sites north of the N340, and often in holiday times, pedestrians are seen to be crossing this very fast and busy 4-lane road by climbing over the barriers to get to the beaches even though footbridges are available. In addition to the pedestrians' deaths, motorists are sometimes killed or injured in the collisions.

Paso de Peatones — Pedestrian Crossing.

UK visitors are used to "Zebra Crossings", where the pedestrian is deemed "never to be at fault". In Spain, the pedestrian is **not** always automatically in the right. Most car drivers will stop if it is safe for them to do so. Scooters / mopeds often do not.

There are basically three similar types of crossings in Spain usually marked with alternate black and white blocks (some have unofficial red / white) painted on the road. They are: -

a) At a road junction, controlled by the same traffic lights as for the vehicles.

b) Controlled by a push-button on the posts at the crossing. (*Espera* means wait) Legally, you should not cross if the "green man" is not lit. Do not cross when the green man is flashing, and hurry if already on the crossing when the sign is.

c) Uncontrolled, with no lights. The traffic is supposed to stop when step onto the crossing and you clearly and positively show drivers the **raised palm of your hand**. Do not assume they will though, especially in the major cities, and do not try to "stop" a fast driver with your hand.

IN ALL CASES, WAIT UNTIL TRAFFIC IS STOPPED COMPLETELY BEFORE CROSSING.

In the villages (*pueblos*) and old the parts of some cities, some streets are closed to through traffic, and are classed as pedestrian streets (*zonas peatonales*).

If there is a footpath (*sendero*) or a pavement (*acero*), pedestrians must use it, although in some villages, old planted trees often block over half the narrow path, causing you to have to walk in the road. Years ago, there were no separate footpaths there.   Do not forget to look the correct way before stepping on the road.   If there are no foot-paths in an area used by pedestrians, then there is generally a speed limit of **12 kph (7 to 8 mph)**

A new Law has come into effect from January 2004, in that pedestrians are not allowed to walk alongside major highways, (defined as autovias / autopistas) except in an emergency such as a car breaking down, in which case it is safer to use a mobile phone.   Motorists will also be fined for stopping to pick up hitchhikers (who will also be fined) on these roads.

After dark on unlit roads, always carry a **good torch** to shine on the road or your legs so the drivers know you are there at the earliest opportunity, and **always face the oncoming traffic**, as in any other country. Most may think you are a policeman waving them down, and most will be cautious because of your torch.   Some of the old mountain roads, especially in the South, are narrow, have no footpaths, and have many blind corners.

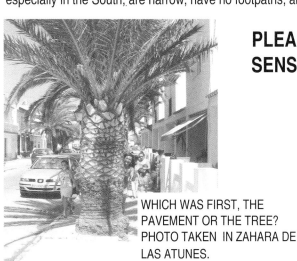

PLEASE USE COMMON SENSE - AND BE SAFE.

WHICH WAS FIRST, THE PAVEMENT OR THE TREE? PHOTO TAKEN IN ZAHARA DE LAS ATUNES.

PART 6-3

Parking.

Parking in the old parts of Spanish towns and villages is often very difficult, especially at holiday times at the coast, and especially if you have a large vehicle. Parking out of town at a railway station where there is usually free parking, or even, if possible, somewhere close to your accommodation and taking a train into the station in the middle of the town, is far more preferable. Fares are very cheap compared with parking and fines. Your car may also be saved from "accidental bump damage".

NOTES ON PARKING ARE: -

1. Car parks, open or underground, or multi-storey. The covered areas offer cool parking for your car in summer, and the peace of mind that you do not have to rush back because you can pay when you leave. If a right-hand drive car, a passenger is useful here to operate the machines, which are on the left hand side of the car when entering and exiting.

2. Pre-paid street parking, **three types**.

2.1 **Blue Zone** (*zona azul*), where the parking bay road markings are in dark blue, and you pay for the ticket at a pay-machine **before** walking away from the car. The pay machine is on the pavement and covers several bays and it is usually signed with a blue background, with a white "P", on the top. **Place the ticket on your dashboard** where it can be seen by the attendants. These bays are only in operation at certain times so read the payment details which, in tourist areas, are often in English also. If you do overstay and receive a fine (*multa*), on some machines, you may be able to clear it easily and quickly by paying €.3 — £1,80 (correct at time of writing) into the parking meter and pressing the correct button to receive a receipt. This is far cheaper than being chased through the post or maybe the car rental agency debiting your credit card.

2,2 **White painted road marking bays**. These are usually free, but in tourist areas, there may be an attendant who will sell you a ticket for usually a €.1. There is no time limit, or if there is, no one usually bothers, including the attendants, who are known as *guardacoches*, and are usually handicapped or retired people earning a living. Beware of beggars posing as attendants.

2.3. Some towns have an **hourly system** (*Hora Zona*), and sell you a coloured ticket denoting 30 min. etc. These can be bought at nearby tobacconists (*estancos* or *tabacs*), and you indicate on the ticket what time you left the car. Do not try to "steal time" as the fines are as if you have overstayed anyway.

4. Some larger towns operate a monthly "season ticket" system at a fixed rate.

You may find an alternating side of the street, parking system, where a blue & red sign (see pages 85 & 86) shows **1 –15** on one side, for the **first 15 days** of the month, and **16—31** on the other side for the second 15 days. The days are when you **cannot park** that side. Look out for these as foreign visitors are often overjoyed to find an empty spot, not wondering why there are no cars on that side already.

6. You may find that some on-street parking bays are "reserved" by a local resident, who has paid for it long term. These are usually marked by black bands on a street post or wall with the car registration on it, and the parked cars will have a card with the same number displayed on the dashboard. Do not park here as it can mean a "towaway" if the owner arrives to use his parking area.

7. A **No Parking Area sign** (*Estacionamiento Prohibido*), where no on-street parking is allowed. It is indicated by a circular sign, blue background, red border, with red diagonal line through it. The sign may have a white arrow painted next to the diagonal, indicating no parking in that direction, and there may also be times shown (24-hour clock type) if the parking is restricted to certain hours. See page 85.

8. As in the UK, **yellow lines** painted on the curb or the road near the curb, also indicate no parking or waiting. A **blue and white curb** is to tell you that you may **wait** briefly but the **driver must stay in the car**.

9. In some villages, the line is painted **white** to indicate the area on the road allowed for pedestrians, often necessary due to the narrow pavements. On the highways (not *autopistas* & *autovias)*, these white lines also indicate pedestrian walkways (in an emergency) or where to stop your car in an emergency **off the road**.

10. If there is a symbol of a tow-truck on the sign, your parked vehicle will be towed away.

11. The access driveways to garages or residential properties may be reserved by the owner, organising this with the local council (*ayuntamiento*), usually for a fee, and there will be a **standard sign** affixed to the gate or door at the entrance. This sign is illustrated on

page 90, in this book. Watch out for these as the owners get **very upset** if you block their access, and your car will be towed or clamped (or worse by the resident) and a fine can also apply.

12. Spaniards, like many other nationalities are always in a hurry (except when you are) in the big cities, and if they cannot park very near their destination, some will anyway and risk a fine if it is for a limited period, such as visiting a shop. The author has witnessed a woman stopping and blocking a busy narrow street in a town during rush hour while she went and bought a loaf of bread. But this can happen anywhere!

13. If you come back to find yourself blocked in your legal parking bay by another car, you may (illegally) blow your horn until the other driver returns. He / she will usually be listening for such a sound.

14. Bogus parking attendants (they "stand out") may approach you for a fee, and you have the choice of telling them to politely "depart", or paying them a small fee to possibly avoid having your paintwork scratched. The author usually **promises** to give something on return if the car is OK, often finding that the phoney attendant has then gone. Neither party has then lost face. Genuine official attendants, often retired persons, have a document supplied by the local council usually worn as a badge, and will give you a numbered receipt from an official pad.

15. **Loading and other reserved bays**. You will see empty parking bays with **zig-zag yellow lines** painted **in the bay**. These bays are for loading at specified times (see the times on the sign-post) or for taxis, ambulances, etc. Parking in these will attract a fine and / or towing away. Also, you may see the zig-zag lines **painted in the road** adjacent to a parking area. This means definitely **NO DOUBLE PARKING.**

EXCMO. AYUNTAMIENTO DE COÍN
SERVICIO DE GRÚA
EL VEHÍCULO MATRÍCULA
HA SIDO RETIRADO POR EL SERVICIO
DE GRÚA Y SE ENCUENTRA EN
EL DEPÓSITO MUNICIPAL
JEFATURA DE LA
POLICIA LOCAL
TEL. 952 45 32 67

Advice sticker left on pavement where a car was illegally parked. It advises that the car (Reg. No. Written on the sticker) can be found at the municipal car pound (or otherwise) and the telephone number to call.

Usually with a Red background colour.

PART 6 - 4

DRIVING LICENCES.

November 2004. On the 9th September, a new law was passed in Spain, bringing the country in line with the EU Directive on the subject. Foreigners with an **EU Card type Driving Licence** may use this licence to drive in Spain, whether a **visitor** or **resident**. However, they must conform to the Spanish Laws as far as renewing the licence is concerned, and these are detailed in this chapter. The older type of Spanish licence is described here out of interest. Please also refer to more details in Part 1 –1, General…

However, the following rules still apply for those with the **pre-card** type licences.

As a **NON-RESIDENT,** if driving any car including a Spanish plated car that **you do not own,**

A. -If you **do not have** one of the new **EU photocard licences complete with paperwork attached**, you will need an **International Driving Licence** (e.g. issued by the AA in the UK), and you must **carry** your **normal licence (I.E. non-photocard)** as well, **OR** ,

B. -An official translation of your driving licence, which can be done for a fee at the Spanish Consulate in your home country. It will be stamped officially as such. **OR,**

C. -for a fee, you may have the translation done by the Spanish Royal Automobile Club (the *RACE*), this certificate being called *Certificado de Equivalencia.*

It is best if you have the "new" EU photo card licence.

You can be fined (up to €450) for failing to carry the correct licence, and the reason for the procedure is so that the Spanish police can easily understand your licence details if you are stopped. The new EU licence cards are standardised and easy to understand whatever language they are in. You will also not be allowed to drive the vehicle away if stopped at a check, and you do not have the correct licence.

DRIVING LICENCES—NON-EU CITIZENS.

Non-EU citizens must have an **International Driver's Licence** issued by their country of normal residence and this will have the Spanish translation included. The following applies if the non-EU citizen wishes to obtain a Spanish Driving Licence. Within the EU, agreements on licences have been made and parity to an acceptable degree with all EU members now agreed. However agreements with many countries **outside of the EU** are still being formulated, although, **for the UK**, there are designated countries as listed below at time of printing.

⇒ The **non-EU** licence cannot be exchanged directly in Spain. However, for certain countries, this is possible **in the UK** if the driver qualifies for a UK licence with certain designated countries listed below. Details can be checked at the **Driver and Vehicle Licensing Agency (DVLA) in the UK**, the web-site is **www.drivers.dvla.gov.uk/drivers**. Or phone **(0044) 870 240 009**. It involves residency in the UK to qualify (see below). You may then use this licence in Spain, but at present, the Spanish authorities will not exchange it for a Spanish one. However, if you have obtain a UK card-type licence, this is not a problem.

DESIGNATED COUNTRIES FOR EXCHANGE OF DRIVING LICENCE FOR UK ONE.

Australia, Barbados, British Virgin Islands, Canada, Hong Kong, Japan, Malta, New Zealand, Cyprus, Singapore, South Africa, Switzerland, and Zimbabwe.

⇒ If the above is not possible, a Spanish driving test must be taken in full. This can cost from €.450 upwards with compulsory driving lessons with a **licensed school** in dual control cars, an official medical **and the test is usually in Spanish,** although some schools on the coasts offer teaching in English, and can arrange the test in English if there is a local demand.

⇒ The test includes eye and reaction testing.

After passing the driving test, you qualify for a B-licence. The "B" licence is probationary and you have to display an "L" plate in the rear window (white with green background) with speed restrictions (80 kph) for one year. Then you can qualify (exchange it) for a full "A" licence.

⇒ The minimum age for a "B" licence for a car (see para 1-1) is 18 to 65 years.

⇒ If you are over 65 when you apply for the Spanish licence, the B-licence procedure does not apply.

⇒ If you are **under 45**, the licence, (including British licences) is re-issued until you are 45, every 10 years after a medical check at the *Trafico* offices, and from 45 to 70, it is renewed **every five years**, unless you drive commercially, then it is to 60 years of age. From 70 years of age, it is renewed (re-approved).every two years, after taking the simple medical test to ensure you are fit to drive.

⇒ You will be refused renewal if you are medically unfit. You may be medically checked at the *Trafico* office location or some registered local clinics in the larger towns. This is an excellent idea used in many other countries to ensure that unfit drivers do not have a "licence to kill" due to bad eyesight or failing health.

⇒ There is no stipulation that as you took the test in an automatic geared car (as you can in the USA), you are not allowed to drive a car with gears, but then, all the driving school cars have gears, and the number of automatic cars on the roads in Spain is very small.

⇒ The Trafico office is open from Monday to Friday, 09H00 to 17H00, except *feria* (fair) and other holidays. However, it is recommended that you phone and check to be sure. It has also been reported that offices are to be opened in other towns such as Torremolinos and Marbella to ease the crowds in the Malaga Trafico offices. These are expected to be confirmed in 2005.

THE SPANISH DRIVING LICENCE AND DRIVING TEST.

It is possible, but difficult if you are not fluent in Spanish, to take the Spanish driving test for a driving licence. There is a theory test, which may be previewed in Spanish on the Trafico web site **www.dgt.es/revista/test/index.html**, a medical to check your eyesight and reactions, and a practical test. Practical learning is carried out in licenced school vehicles equipped with dual foot controls with a government registered instructor. There are licensed schools that can give instruction in English and can arrange to have the test taken in English where the demand calls for it, i.e. the Costa del Sol and Costa Blanca.

There are schools that can give instruction in English where the demand calls for it, i.e. the Costa del Sol and Costa Blanca. The existing licence (the one shown below (*Permiso de Conducción*) was issued in May 2003) is intended to be easy to understand in most countries in the EU. The vehicles covered by the licence are pictured with the weights or capacities, and the date on which the licence for each class of vehicle expires.

Sample Pre-EU Card-Type Spanish Driving Licence.

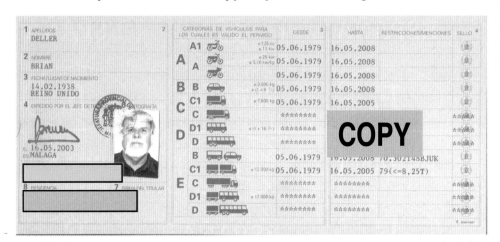

SPANISH HEADING	ENGLISH TRANSLATION
1. Apellidos del titular.	Last Name / s.
2. Nombre.	First name.
3. Plaza y fecha de nacimiento	Country / Place and date of birth
4. Expedido por el jefe de trafico.	Place and date of licence issue with official signature of *Trafico* official.
5. Numero del permiso.	Licence number, usually the same as Spanish issued national identity number (NIE / NIF).
6. Domicilio de conductor.	Photograph and *Trafico* stamp.
7. Firma de Titular.	Signature of holder.
8. Residencia	Holder's home address.

The right hand side of the card shows what the driver is licensed to drive, with the column titled "*hasta*" (until) being the dates that the licence expires.

Eventually, the **author is of the opinion** that all EU licences will eventually be replaced by a magnetic card with the above information printed on it and the feature so that the police can "swipe" it through a portable PC to speed Law enforcement via the main computers, even while patrolling on the road. This is a good idea to eliminate the drivers who are banned from driving, but ignore the ban, even using forged licences.

List of some *Trafico* Forms

When you arrive at the *Trafico* Office, you must first get the form for the service you require. Go to the *Información* counter and ask for: -

TASA 2,4	Solicitud de canje del permiso de conducción	Application for driving licence, including renewals.
TASA 4.1	Solicitud de datos del Registro de vehiculs	Application to see vehicle details.
TASA 1,5 or 4,1	Solicitud de transmission.	Transfer of ownership

TASA 4,4	Solicitud de Duplicado de:
	-Permiso de Conducción
	    -Licencia de Conducción
	    -Permiso de Circulación
	    -Licencia de Circulacion
		Application for duplicates of vehicle and driving licences.

If you are transferring ownership, you will need a completed **Form 620**, which is obtained at a *tabac* (tobacconists shop) or at the *Hacienda*, and actioned at the *Hacienda* tax offices, as described in Part 10 – 2 in this book.

Traffic fines (*multas*) can also be paid at the *Trafico* or by post with postal orders.

El Trafico Office, - How to Navigate the "Sea of Faces".

A visit to especially the Malaga *Trafico* office is an experience, especially on a hot summer's day when the air-conditioning does not cope with the many hot bodies queuing for the various services, but the staff are very nice and helpful, even if your Spanish is not good, and if you **have plenty of time**, you can get to your objective. However, if you are in a hurry or cannot afford the day off work, use a *gestor*. There are people outside the offices looking for foreigners and others not familiar with the procedure to assist for a price, but their charges are such that you are better off using a *gestor,* especially when you add your travel costs to the bill.

Virtually none of the *trafico oficina* staff can speak English, and **why should they?**

You will/may need to use the *Oficina del Trafico* to: -

a.   Obtain / change your driving licence.

b.   Register a **change of ownership** of a vehicle. If you have bought new or used from a Dealer, they will do this for you.

c.   Pay a **fine** (multa).

d.   Register your **change of address**. Be careful here because in some towns in Malaga, you can do this at your town hall (*ayuntimiento*). Ask a neighbour. This should be done within 10 days of change.

e.   To **obtain duplicates** or alter the details on your vehicle documents, e.g. the *permiso de circulation.*

There are fees to pay, but these are reasonable when compared with other countries, usually (in Malaga) €.16,40 for an original licence and €.7 for a copy at time of publication.

Web site information.

The author's Web site contains **ongoing information gained after the publishing of this edition of the book**. It may be viewed at

www.spainvia.com/motoringinspain.htm

If you have any comments, please E-mail the author at
viadevida@spainvia.com

Summary Note. As per the EU Directive, since 9th September, 2004, the Law has been changed in Spain so that foreign EU citizens with a "new" card-type licence are now able to drive in Spain using their EU card type licences issued in another EU country. The Laws as applicable to Spanish Driving Licences do apply though, and the reader should be familiar with this fact.
The Laws are noted in this chapter, Part 6—4.

Part 6-5

MUNICIPAL VEHICLE TAX (ROAD TAX?).

Owners of Spanish registered cars and motorcycles must pay a tax similar to the Road Fund Licence in the UK and many other countries, to the local Town Hall or *Ayuntimiento*. The amount varies from town to town, that is, it is not nationally set at a fixed rate. There is no receipt to be displayed on your car's windscreen: however, you should keep a copy of it, an A4 paper form, with the other papers in your glove compartment. As an example, for a car of the size of a Ford Focus 1750 cc, the tax may be about €.121 per year. The amounts vary according to the horsepower of the vehicle and are listed each year in my web site.

It is called the "***Impuesto municipal sobre vehículos de tracción mecanica***".

As a foreigner, you must also register with your local town hall, and you will need your NIE paper form or *residencia* card, and a copy of your proof of residence, such as a property rental contract for at least one year, or ownership of property paper copies, all in the area administered by the town hall. The cost is minimal, about €.2, or £1,40 (some do not charge at all) and you will be issued with the **Nota de Empadronamiento** confirming the residence in that area, and, the council **will welcome your application**. This *nota* is re-issued each year, usually free of charge (you must collect it) and the town hall welcomes this registering because they qualify for financial allowances from the Province based on total population in their area.

Payment of the local "road tax" is made before May each year, and there can be a discount if you pay early or on time, and a "fine" if you pay late, usually 5% for the first month, then 20% for succeeding months.

If you move your address into another council area, you will need to advise the *Trafico* of this move and have it changed on your driving licence, etc. Unlike many countries, you cannot always do it at the local council or police offices as you need to register it through the Provincial Traffic Office. So a move to Marbella may mean advising the office in Malaga, either personally, or through a *gestor*, etc. This is unusual in these days of computer networks, where registering at one office in a Province, or even country, means that the main records files are automatically updated. However, it has been announced that Trafico offices are expected to be opened in Marbella, Torremolinos and maybe Estepona in 2.005. Already the hours of business have been extended to 5 pm to cope with the ever increasing work load.

If you go yourself for any changes, payments, or licence details at the *Trafico,* **go to the information desk for the correct form first.**, and remember to take a paper **number tag** from the machine to book your place in the queue.

You cannot sell or trade in your car without the latest *impuesto* (local road tax) receipt being presented during the transfer of ownership.

Part 6 - 6

MOTORCYCLES – SOME OBSERVATIONS.

I love motorcycles, having owned and ridden them, including club racing and sprinting on tarmac, foot-ups and off-road long-distance enduros (some over 150 miles [242 km] in the USA), for over forty years.   Spain has an ideal climate for them, especially on the coasts, as Madrid gets cold in the winter and sometimes there is slight snow, but nothing like northern Europe.   However, there are not that many large capacity motorcycles here possibly due to the high cost of purchase and insurance, but the towns are crowded with scooters and mopeds and lately, quadricycles (four-wheel motorcycles), ridden in most cases by "kamikaze pilots", who swerve all over the road, jump or ignore traffic lights and Stop street-signs, and often add to the high accident rates amongst this class of rider.

As a result of the seemingly impossible task of reducing the law-breaking and accident rates for the young riders, the age of first licence has been raised from 14 to 16 in 2.004.

On the coasts, especially in summer, many do not use crash helmets and often ride in "flip-flop" sandal shoes, no gloves, bare-chested (not the girls: well, not yet), and especially with no eye-protection.   As someone who has been a volunteer instructor with the RAC / ACU Motorcycle Training Scheme in the UK, and with a similar organisation in South Africa where we taught even the local traffic police at one time, I feel very strongly that not only the authorities but parents must take urgent action to instil self-discipline in these, quite frankly, foolish youths.   After all, if you are involved in an accident with one, especially as a foreigner, your insurance, if you are covered, can be awarded high cost penalties / damages if it can be proved that you were at fault at all, and if your cover is not sufficient, you must pay out of your pocket.   You also have to use a local lawyer; —more costs. Often, the rider may find witnesses to prove you were wrong as he / she lives there.

Occasionally when complaints reach a high level, the local police will have a "blitz", and organise roadblocks, confiscating machines (until the fault is corrected) that are very noisy (common complaint) or where riders do not have a crash helmet.   It is not unusual to see riders tearing around with their crash helmet hooked on their arm or on the back carrier.

They say that it is too hot to wear them, even in winter! Childish rebellion!

The few large machine riders you see often ride at high speeds (180 – 200 kph? Or 110 to 122 mph) along the four-lane *carreteras, autopistas* and *autovias* but you do not see the number of serious accidents that the other mopeds and scooter riders are involved in.

Dipped headlights must be used at all times by motorcyclists with engines over 49 cc, although surveys in the USA has proved that other road users still claim "to not see them". Children must be at least **seven** years of age, to ride on a bike with a parent, and if with another adult (not the parent), **written authorisation** must be supplied by the parents, which the other adult must then carry.

You can rent motorcycles of all sizes in Spain, although it is not cheap, but for a day out on an automatic scooter to a Honda Goldwing, (a 1500 cc six-cylinder moto, more a two-wheeled car) the cost can be justified on a holiday: - if you are confident about riding on the **right** side of the road.   The *caveats* when renting are the same as with a car. Make sure **all** prior damage is recorded, tyres are in **very good** condition and **correctly inflated**, and if you do not have a crash helmet, one will be provided. Best to have your own. The rental insurance does not always include theft, so be careful and ask exactly what it does cover, because you may be asked to leave something of value such as your passport with the rental company, (although this is, strictly speaking, illegal) and if the bike is stolen, you will have great difficulty in getting it back until you pay the costs.   And theft is a problem, although no worse than anywhere else in Europe. Bikes are supplied with security chains.

A Spanish or resident teenager with a local licence can ride a moped up to 49 cc and 60 kph top speed without a driving licence, but they must have insurance, although local Press reports state that about 25% of these younger riders have no insurance at all. Foreigners are restricted to the ages stated on their driving licences. If you have a car licence, this is sufficient to ride a moped or 49 cc scooter. For all other machines over this size, a motor-cycle driving licence is needed as well as at least Third Party insurance, which can be expensive for reasons stated above.   Many Spanish insurance companies are now unwilling to insure these young riders without expensive premiums because of the accident rates. Details are in Part 1-1.

Spain really needs a national incentive for road safety and skills training for these young riders, and it needs to be insisted upon by the parents, as well as all the authorities. Loving Spain as I do, I have to admit that in many ways they have a way to go to catch up, as the accident rates prove, compared with, for example, the UK, where the excellent RAC / ACU Training Scheme was in operation some thirty plus years ago.

As a point of interest, the generic word in Spanish for motorcycle and scooter is "moto", and when this word is used in other contexts, it also means "**in a rush**" and "**to get really turned on sexually**".   No wonder the Spanish love their motos.

MODIFIED MOTOR-CYCLES (MOTOS).

As in other EU countries, it is illegal to modify your moto unless it is approved by the manufacturer and the EU regulations.   When you look around the Spanish cities at all the noisy scooters with modified exhausts, especially four-wheeled ATV's, and many obviously with hotted-up engines, you wonder if the law is enforced.   New proposals are that motos are to be thoroughly checked for this point when they go for the ITV or MOT test. However, as motos are not liable for this test until they are five years old, there is plenty of leeway in the meantime.   What is does mean is that if you are buying a second-hand machine, it is important that you have it tested and accepted by the testing ITV authority before you pay over the cash, especially if it is a private sale, as you may have to buy a new exhaust system to pass the test.

In practice, the larger modern motos are so close in performance to their racing counterparts used on the track, it is unnecessary to do much to improve them and most are quieter than small cars.   After all, how fast do you want to go, when the larger sports motos already have 250 kph plus top speeds, with acceleration times that will leave Ferraris, etc. behind up to 160 kph.

PART 7—1

ROAD SIGNS IN SPAIN.

A comparison of the Spanish road-signage shows that there are many more than in say the British Highway Code book. No wonder it takes a long time to learn them all, and visitors from the UK and Ireland, where there are far fewer different signs, are at a loss when they see many of them.

Many of the road signs in Spain are common to adjoining countries on the Continent. Perhaps one day, the EU will be standardised in this matter, but until then **it is vital** that foreign drivers unused to the differences aquaint themselves with the Spanish signs to speed travelling, save wasting time but most important to **avoid accidents** and / or **stiff fines** for not obeying a sign.

While the Spanish police are understanding to a certain degree, it is no defence to state that you are a foreigner and do not know the signs. Ignorance is no excuse in Spain, as in any other country where the driver is privileged to use a motor vehicle. **The author has questioned British drivers who have lived here years, and drive every day, on the meaning of some fairly common signs, and discovered that they did not know what they meant! A few have refused to buy this book because "I live here!"**

The following pages show signs that are peculiar to Spain, and some that are universal on the Continent. It is repeated as it is very important that you familiarise yourself with them. **You may save a fine, - or far worse.**

They cover: -

- Priority signs, where you are told what to do for safety's sake.
- Obligatory signs: you must obey them.
- End of obligation area signs where you return to the previous rule.
- Danger (*peligroso*) signs. Warning you of the need for caution ahead.
- Prohibition signs. You "cannot do that here!"
- General indication signs; e g "*Autovia* from this point"

- **Vertical board** signs are where temporary notices are placed on a pole to show the current state of the road ahead, especially in mountain areas where the weather can change quickly.
- Lane signs. Your lane may end ahead or a new lane start.
- Service signs.
- Direction signs.
- Confirmation follow-up signs.
- Officially approved (homulgamated) information signs.
- Colour coding of various urban advice signs: what they mean.
- Road works signs.

Please note that the author has abbreviated: -

"Motorcycles" to the Spanish "**motos**" , and, No Entry to **N/E** — to save space.

CAUTION. Example of a roundabout (*rotunda* or *glorieta*) with a "Give Way (*cedo el paso*)" on it to give preference to traffic coming **OFF** the *autovia* from the **right** . The road painting is almost worn away, but the sign is intact. **Potential accident point for the unwary**. Normally, traffic coming from **your left on** the roundabout has priority .

Priority Signs.

You have priority (right of way) to proceed.

End of your priority area.

You <u>must</u> give way to traffic from other direction.

If needed, give way to the other driver, (red arrow). Road is usually very narrow at this point for a bridge, etc.

Give Way? Can have symbol in triangle or on a white rectangular sign below to qualify why.

Universal, **must STOP** sign.

One way this direction. Several variations of this sign.

Cambio de Sentido. Change of direction. (over/under bridge?).

Cars & small trucks may use this lane. Not motos **without** sidecars

Mounted animals (horses, etc), use this lane.

Pedestrians may walk here.

All signs with a blue background and a round, thick red border are
"you must do" signs.
Round and with blue background are **advice** signs.

Motocycles may use this lane except with sidecar.

All trucks may use this lane.

Bicycles may us this lane.

Horse-drawn vehicles may use this lane.

Minimum speed from this point.

Fit snow chains if needed. (Penalty fine if stuck).

Drive on dipped lights. Usually through a tunnel.

Lane for trucks with all dangerous cargos.

Lane for vehicles carrying 3.000 litres plus of dangerous liquids.

Lane for for vehicles carrying explosive or inflammable cargos.

Use of seatbelts (all, where fitted) obligatory.

End of advised minimum speed limit area.

End of Prohibition Signs. Black on White backgrounds.

End of a prohibition area.

End of speed restricted area, eg 60 kph.

End "no overtaking" area.

End of "no overtaking by trucks" area.

End of limited parking area.

Sign not shown, End of no horn-blowing area.

GENERAL ADVICE SIGNS.

Start of Autopista.

Start of Autovia.

Start of "Fast Road".

End of Autopista.

End of Autovia.

Note. "Via Rapida" signs are being phased out in 2004.

End of "Fast Road".

Road for cars & motos only.

End of road for cars & motos.

Tunnel ahead.

End of tunnel.

Advised speed.

Advised speed ends.

Area with **advised** speed range, start / finish.

One way street.

All lanes one way. Can be 2 or three plus.

Road ahead is one-way to the right (or left, etc, as applicable).

Pedestrian crossing ahead.

| Pedestrian underpass ahead. | Pedestrian bridge ahead. | Advance warning of no through road. | No through road to left, (or ahead or right as applicable). |

Bus or Tram stops ahead.

Public parking available here.

Taxi rank.

End of dipped headlights area.

Emergency telephone on highway.

You may change direction (*Cambio de Sentido*) 300 m ahead.

Entering/leaving a residencial area with children playing, etc. hazards.
20 kph (12 mph) maximum speed.
Maybe no footpaths?

Exit slip roads signs to gauge distances when leaving autovias and autopistas.

PROHIBITION SIGNS. (Note N/E = No Entry)

No traffic at all allowed.

No entry.

N/E to cars & motos.

N/E , cars & trucks.

N/E to motos.

No entry to mopeds.

No entry to agricultural vehicles.

N/E to mounted horses.

Narrow Road (in metres).

No trucks at all.

No trucks over shown weight.

No entry for trucks carrying dangerous products

No entry to vehicles carrying explosive substances.

No entry to carriers of 3.000 litres plus of dangerous liquids.

N/E to vehicles with a towed

N/E animal drawn vehicles.

N/E to bicycles.

N/E to vehicles moved by hand.

N/E to pedestrians.

Limited height (in metres).

Minimum following distance.

Maximum Speed.

PROHIBITION SIGNS, CONTINUED.

Vehicle must stop here for reason given on another sign.

Maximum all up weight limit.

Maximum weight limit per axle.

Maximum vehicle length.

Only Toll Road this way.

No entry to vehicles with trailers, except semi-trailers (articulated).

No left (or right, if other way) turn.

No "U"-turn.

No overtaking.

No horn sounding zone.

No parking on this side of road on odd dates. (1st, 3rd, etc).

Trucks, 3.500 kg plus, not allowed to overtake.

No parking or stopping.

No parking.

No parking on this side of road on even dates (2nd,4th,6th,etc).

Limited time (shown) parking zone.

81

| No parking 1st-15th of each month. | No parking 16th to 31st of each month. | Sample signs seen at **ROADWORKS**. Similar to other types but with yellow background. |

DANGER SIGNS.

All these signs show that **you have priority** over the other road users exiting the minor junctions.

You must **GIVE PRIORITY** to vehicles coming from your **RIGHT**. **(This is an important sign to know).**

Traffic lights ahead.

Roundabout/traffic circle ahead. Give way to your **LEFT**, unless otherwise signed.

Tramway crossing ahead. **They** have priority.

Caution! "Opening" bridge ahead.

DANGER SIGNS (Cont.).

Level crossing with gates ahead

Level crossing NO gates. **Caution.**

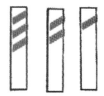

Distance markers, on the **RIGHT SIDE OF ROAD**, to opening bridge or level crossing.

Distance markers, on the **LEFT SIDE OF ROAD**, to opening bridge or level crossing.

1—track. 2—tracks.

Warning signs of immediate presence of a level crossing **WITHOUT** a barrier.

Aircraft fly low over road ahead.

Dangerous curve to right (or left).

Dangerous curves, both ways, ahead, as shown.

Road works ahead.

Steep hill ahead—**DOWN.**

Steep hill ahead—**UP.**

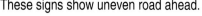

These signs show uneven road ahead.

Narrowing of road, as indicated.

Road can be slippery.

DANGER SIGNS. (Cont.).

Pedestrian
crossing ahead.

Pedestrians (children)
in area and no
footpaths.

Bicycle crossing
area.

Caution, free
ranging domestic
animals.

Wild animals may
be on road.

Traffic runs in both directions
Sometimes a temporary sign
on dual carriageway after an
accident.

Obstacles(?) on road.

Loose gravel on
road.

Road ends at
quayside.

Level drop on side of
road as indicated.

Strong
cross
winds.

Obstruction on
highway ahead.

Poor visibility
ahead.

Usually traffic
congestion
ahead.

Be aware of other
dangers!

Road very
slippery when
snowing or icy.

SPEED LIMITS IN SPAIN

Unless otherwise signposted..

 Urban areas—50 kph (30 mph).

 Main two-way roads– 90 kph (55 mph).

  Via Rapidas– 100 kph (62 mph). Via Rapidas are being discontinued during 2004.

 Autovias and Autopistas– 120 kph (74 mph).

 On Auto-roads showing exit ahead with exit number

 Distance (in metres) to exit. Usually shown with above exit sign.

 Sign at exit point. Usually with other white background sign showing where you can go to by taking this exit. Also used on carreteras with a distance sign.

500 m Distance sign used on carreteras with other signs.

 Signs on Autopista/via showing Exit 223, with route to the N-623 to Santander. Exit here at this point on slip road.

PLEASE NOTE THAT THE ABOVE SPEED LIMITS ARE THE MAXIMUM. CERTAIN VEHICLES HAVE LOWER LIMITS DEPENDING ON THEIR TYPE AND CONFIGURATION AS DESCRIBED ON PAGE 29.

MORE SIGNS YOU WILL ALSO SEE.

Signs indicating you **must not** make a **direct** left turn, but there is a turn right slip lane where you may then safely turn150 metres (about 150 yards) ahead. You may also go back in the direction you are now travelling.

SOS Telephones.
These are placed approximately 1—2 km apart on major highways. Press the button and ask for help. There is a recorded message in four languages. Leave your details and location and (eventually) you will be reached.

Sign placed on garage doors or gates (often at private residences) to advise road users **not to block access at any time**.

"Garage entrance. Keep permanently clear".

Maximum speed 40 kph (25 mph). .

A SIGN WITH A
YELLOW
BACKGROUND
INDICATES
TEMPORARY
ROADWORKS.

PART 7-2

Common Road Sign Types.

Description of Sign	Type
Triangle, white background, red border, black symbol/letters.	**Warning!**
Triangle **inverted** white background, red border and sometimes black symbol/letters.	Give way? You must note & obey!
Sign with yellow background, black border and symbol or letters. Different shapes and sizes.	**Road works** (*Obras*) Temporary signs similar to all other normal ones.
Circle, white background, red border, black symbol/letters.	You must note & obey!
Circle, blue background, red symbol	You must note & obey!
Circle, white background, black symbol/letters.	You must note & obey!
Rectangular sign, blue background with white letters	Advice on Autopista and Autovia roads
Signs with green backgrounds and white letters, and some with white background and black letters.	"Via Rapida" roads. Being phased out in 2004.
Vertical Boards. These are usually temporary advice signs with a white background, attached to poles. The advice varies with the weather.	Mountain areas, usually.

 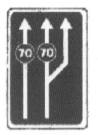  

Lanes shown with minimum speeds in good conditions.

Lane reserved for buses only. You may cross only at a road-junction.

These signs show closing/opening of lanes on a highway.

 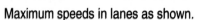   

Maximum speeds in lanes as shown.

Must take direction in lane as shown. One lane straight on after this junction.

HIGHWAY (AUTOPISTA, AUTOVIA,) SIGNS.
White on blue background, red borders.

Signs showing lane directions ahead.

SERVICE SIGNS.

First Aid ahead.

Emergency
treatment
ahead.

Licensed vehicle
test station.
(MOT test?)

Repair
facilities.

Public
telephone.

Fuel ahead.

Fuel ahead,
all types.

Fuel and
repairs

Camping, tents only.

Camping, caravans & tents.

Hotel or motel.

Restaurant.

Cafeteria.

Land for caravan camping/parking.

Snack bar.

Departure point for hiking.

Rest area.

Youth hostel.

Tourist information.

Fishing preserve.

Train station with parking.

Underground train station with parking.

Bus station with parking.

Train	Bus stop.	Bus stop.	Tram stop.	Airport.
Arrivals.	Departures.	Heliport.	Port.	Car Ferry.
Water fount.	Wild animals.	Park.	Pier/Jetty.	Museum.
Castle.	Football Stadium.	Workshop.	Fuel Station.	Fuel supply, all types.
Campsite, Tents.	Campsite, Caravans.	Viewpoint	Picnic spot.	Hiking trail.

OFFICIALLY APPROVED INFORMATION SIGNS.

Close to site. Black on white background. You may also see many of these signs in white on blue background showing you the way to these sites.

Fishing.

Bull Fight Ring.

Funicular railway.

Pedestrian zone. No paths?

Children in area.

(Guess?)

Fish factory.

Supermarket.

Car rentals.

Car wash.

National monument.

Beach.

Bar or cafeteria.

Pharmacy.

Restaurant.

Town centre.

Toilets.

Exit here. (Highway).

Inhabited area.

Cemetery.

No hard shoulders.

Road has hard-shoulders.

Industrial area.

Pottery factory.

Handicapped persons.

Hospital.	First Aid. Red Cross!	Post Office. (*Correos*)	Fire risk.area.	Youth hostel.

Parador. These are old buildings of some splendour that have been modernised by the Spanish government and used as at least 4-star hotels.   Pensioners get a discount.

Parador de Turismo. As above but especially equipped and intended for tourists.

Albergue. A hotel usually in a remote area. Similar to a youth hostel.

Theatre.	Amusement Park.	Public telephone.	Snow or Ice.

Cable car.

Sports ground.

NEW SIGNS January 2004.

The signs and information on the next four pages have been issued by the Spanish Department of the Interior in 2003-04 as part of the ongoing campaign to improve road safety and reduce accidents in Spain.   Included in the changes are: -

⇒   The removal of the classification and signs for "Via Rapidas".   These signs, rectangular with white symbols on a green background, as shown on page 82, have been left in this book, as it will be some time before they are all removed from the roads, for the information of readers and when reading other literature printed before issue of this book.

⇒   Please note that the police often have a football-type whistle to attract your attention.

⇒   It has also been advised in the Press that the police forces are buying more speed monitoring radar equipment.

Police signal. With arm raised vertically, you must safely **STOP** until signalled to proceed in the direction indicated by the policeman on point duty. Usually the way youwish to gothrough the junction. **Do not enter the road junction** until signalled to by the officer.

Police signal. With arm, or both, arms held horizontally, all traffic is to **STOP** approaching the front and rear of the policeman.

Rocking a **red** or **yellow hand held light**. You must safely **STOP** and then move in the direction indicated by the policeman's arm and the light.

Continued >

SIGNALS FROM OFFICIAL VEHICLES.

 **Red** flag or signal. **Follow** the police motor-cycle, or STOP if other signs indicate this action.

 **Green** flag or signal. You may now safely **pass** the police motor-cycle as the road is now open and clear.

 **Yellow** flag or signal. Take **extreme caution** in that area as there is a particular danger there (usually an accident or road works etc.).

 Left arm extended and moved up and down from the elbow. You must **safely STOP** on the right hand side of the road behind the police officer.

 Flashing red or yellow light. You must safely move to the right hand side of the road and **STOP**.

Continued >

NEW SIGNS, 2004.

Pedestrian area. They have precedence.

No entry for mopeds.

Turning left prohibited

Bicycle way reserved for cyclists.

Way reserved for mopeds (with pedals).

End of reserved way for cycliosts.

Start of lane for cars and motos.

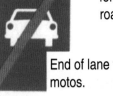
End of lane for cars and motos.

No Entry. Way exclusively for use by toll road officials.

ZONA 30

Maximum speed 30 kph (18 mph) zone with **pedestrians having priority.**

Service area with services available.

Bicycles must stay in right hand lane.

Way ahead is OK cycles. (Green background).

 senda ciclable 5

Way/road suitable for cycling. Usually a scenic route. "5" shows 5 km in this case.

Service area ahead, 500 metres, with services available indicated.

Vertical board signs showing potential hazards ahead.

 Snow.

 Heavy rain.

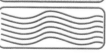 Flooding.

Cycle lane only. **Painted on the road**.

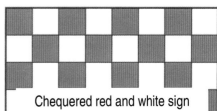

Chequered red and white sign **painted on the road** indicates an emergency braking zone ahead (for heavy trucks?). No stopping or parking allowed.

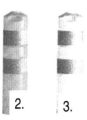

1.   2.   3.

These "soft" bollards indicate: - 1. The presence of a temporary curve: 2. Road works limits: 3. Other obstacles.

ertical board
gns seen on
nountain roads.

Advice sign usually In mountain areas. Blocked roads; fallen rocks or snow , etc.

.BIERTO	OPEN
RUDENCIA	CAUTION
ECAUCIÓN	EXTRA CAUTION
PELIGRO	DANGER
ERRADO	CLOSED

Trucks, not allowed to overtake

No trucks & 60 kph max. Speed.

Signs showing advised and "must do" direction of driving at a junction.

Max. Weight 3,5 tonnes & chains may be needed for snow.

Part 7—2.

Translations of Common Notices seen on Signs.

Spanish	English	Advice
2 (?) m	Two (?) meters	Indicates distance. Just over two yards. 1m = about 3,2 feet.
Abierto	Open.	
Acceso solo	Access only	Cannot get out here.
Aeropuerto	Airport	
Aparcamiento	Parking	Also, *Estacionamiento.*
ATENCIÓN – USO MOTOR COMO FRENO	Warning, Use engine as a brake.	Select a low gear to save brakes overheating. Usually before very steep and long inclines.
Autobus	Coach / Omnibus	
Autoservicio	Self-service	
Barrera e Seguridad	Security barrier	ARMCO or concrete, etc.
Bombero / s	Fireman / men	On a sign in a reserved parking area?
Cadenas para la Nieve.	Snow Chains.	**(If needed)** Sign shows tyre with chains fitted.
Calle de sentido.	One way street.	Usually on round sign, black horizontal line on white circle with red border.

Cambio de Sentido.	**Change of Direction.** Sign indicates whether you go over or under the highway you are on.	Where you may turn over / under a highway and go back the way you came. Signs are rectangular, **Blue background**, **White lettering**, giving warning of turn off ahead, and **White background, Black lettering** at turn-off point.
Camíon/es	Truck/s	
Carretera cerrado.	Road closed	
Cerrado.	Closed.	Used everywhere.
Coche.	Car	
Control de Galibo.	Police check point for vehicle condition and papers.	This is where you hope all is well with your vehicle and documents.
Curva/s Peligrosa/s.	Dangerous Curve / s.	Triangle, white background, red border and black symbol.
Desvío.	Detour or Diversion.	
........Desprendimientos	Loosening (of road) ahead.	Road has a (temporaray) bad surface.
Derecha.	Right	
Entrada	Entrance	

Fin (de zona, prohibition, etc)	End (of restriction, etc.)	
Furgón & furgoneta.	A van (or wagon) & a small van.	
Gasolinera	Petrol Station	
Glorieta	Roundabout	
GRUA	Breakdown truck or crane.	If needed, you can use this word when asking for help.
Guia	Guide	
Izquierda	Left	
"L" plates in rear window of a car. (**Driving schools** have a blue background, white L-plate usually on the roof of car).	**Learner/probationer**. "B" licence holder. Plates are white "L" on green background. Usually inside the rear window.	After a driver has passed the test, there is a year "on probation" with certain restrictions e.g. 80 kph maximum speed limit.
Peaje	Toll Road.	Sometimes also has "**Toll**" as well on sign.
Playa	Beach	Indicates way to beach.
Poligono Industrial, or Zona Industrial.	Commercial District, usually factories and larger storage buildings.	Area where only businesses are situated.
Póngase en el carril.	Stay or get in (correct) lane.	
Puente bajo	Low bridge	
Puerta	Door	House, car, etc.
Puerto (de mar)	Sea Port.	
Red	Net (work)	As in Road network.

Ruta alternativo.	Alternative route.	
Salida de Camiones.	Exit (also entrance?) for heavy trucks.	Usually warning of a **construction site** access point.
Salida.	Exit.	
Semáforas.	Traffic lights.	
SP, (Servicio Publico).	Public Service.	"SP" sign on back of taxis, etc.
Via (de Servicios?).	Way (to toilets, etc).	
Libre.	Open to public. (vacancies?).	Usually for a car park.
La primera quincena del mes.	The first two weeks of the month.	Often seen on parking signs for parking on different sides of a road.
La segunda quincena del mes.	The second two weeks of the month.	As above.
Transporte escolar.	School bus.	
Via Rapida.	Fast Road ("fast way"). Not a motorway.	A two- way single road, usually no centre barriers, wider than normal, good surface and intended to be for fast travel up to speeds of 90 kph or as posted.

Part 8-1

Translation of Words Associated with Motoring – Spanish to English & English to Spanish.

PLEASE NOTE.

In Spanish, as with all the Latin based languages, nouns are either male or female, so the item's definite article, "the" in Spanish is either; male-single "**el**": female-single "**la**", male-plural "**los**", female-plural "**las**". If there is a mixture of male and female, the word used is "**los**". In this table, after each of the above Spanish nouns, the gender is identified as a help. **The pronunciation of the words is not covered here. If this is a problem, show this book to the Spanish person to help you explain what you need.**

SPANISH	ENGLISH
Acabado (adj)	Finish (paintwork, etc).
Aceite (el)	Oil
Acelarador (el)	Accelerator
Acero (el) — & adjective.	Steel, (as in llanta de acero—steel wheel).
Acero inoxidable	Stainless steel
Aire/Agua	Air/water
Aleación (de ruedas)	Alloy (wheels)
Alimentación (la)	Fuel system. (Feed system)
Alineación	Alignment (wheels)
Altavoz	Speaker (radio)
Alternador (el)	Alternator
Amortiguador/es (el)	Shock absorber/s
Ancho (adj.)	Wide

Spanish	English
Anillo (el)	Ring
Antibloqueo	ABS (brakes)
Anticongelante (el)	Antifreeze
Anti-niebla (Faros)	Fog lights
Antirobbo	Anti-theft
Aparcamiento (el): Aparcar en doble fila	Car park: Double-parking
Arbol de levas (el)	Camshaft
Arbol de transmisión	Drive shaft
Asiento delantro/trasero	Seat front/rear
Averia (la)	Breakdown
Ayudas (la)	Assistance aids, ABS/ESB, etc.
Banda (la)	Tread (tyre)
Bastidor (el)	Chassis
Bateria (la)	Battery
Bicicleta de montaña (la)	Mountain bike
Biela (Bieletta) (la)	Connecting rod (small connecting rod)
Bloque y Culata	Block (engine) and head (cylinder).
Bobina (la)	(Ignition) coil
Bocina or Pito or Klaxon (el)	Horn
Bomba (la)	Pump
Botella para el agua (la)	Water bottle
Bujía (la)	Spark plug
Cable (el)	Cable
Cadena (la)	Chain

Spanish	English
Cadenas para la nieve.	Snow chains
Caja de cambios (la)	Gearbox
Calentador. (el)	Heater
Camara. (la)	Inner tube
Cambio automática. (el)	Automatic gearbox
Cambio de marcha (el)	Gear-change (stick).
Camión (el): Camionero	Truck: truck-driver
Capó. (el)	Bonnet/Hood
Caravana. (la)	Caravan
Carburador. (el)	Carburettor
Cargador de bateria	Battery charger
Carnet de Conducir. (el)	Driving licence (also Permiso de Conducción)
Carrocería	Bodywork
Carrocero/a (el/la)	Panel-beater
Cárter (de cigüeñal)	Housing (....crankcase, oil sump)
Casco (el)	Crash-helmet
Casco (el) de moto	Helmet, motorcycle.
Catafaras (el)	Reflector (car)
Catalizador (el)	Catalytic Converter
Ciclomoto ((el)	Moped
Cierre centrolizado (el)	Central locking.
Cigüeñal	Crankshaft
Cilindrada	Capacity (Engine, cc)
Cinturón de seguridad (el)	Seat-belt

Spanish	English
Coche (el): coche automatico	Car: Automatic (transmission) car
Cojinete (el) (de bolas) (de rodillos).	Bearing. (ball) (roller).
Columna de dirección (el)	Steering column
Combustible 95 or 98 Sin plomo gasolina 97 gasolina Gasoleo *or* diesel	**Fuel** 95 or 98 octane non-lead 97 Lead replacement petrol. Diesel.
Consumo (medio o mixto) (el)	Fuel consumption (average) (l/100km?)
Contrapeso	Balance weight (wheel)
Control de velocidad	Speed trap.
Correa del aircondicianado (la)	Air-con. drive belt
Correa de la distribución. (la)	Belt, drive, (toothed) for cylinder head valves.
Correa del servodirección (la)	Power-steering drive belt
Correa del ventilador (la)	Fan belt
Cotas	Figures (eg, bore and stroke)
Cremallera y piñón	Rack and pinion (Steering?)
Cuadro (el)	Frame
Cuatro tiempo	Four-stroke
Cuentakilómetros (el)	Odometer (distance recorder on speedometer)
Cuero (el)	Leather
Culato	Cam cover
Delantera	Front (adjective)
Deportivo (el), coche	Sport (-car).
Deposito de liquido	Reservoir

Spanish	English
Depòsito del combustible. (el)	Fuel tank
Dirección (la)	Steering.
Dirección asistida (la)	Power-steering.
Disco (el)	Disk e.g. Brake.
Distribuidor (el)	Distributor
Distribución ((la)	Delivery, usually type of cylinder head.
Dos tiempo	Two-stroke
Eje (de rueda) (el)	Axle (wheel)
Elevalunas eléctrico (los)	Electric Windows (up/down).
Embotellamiento (el)	Traffic jam
Embrague (el)	Clutch
Encendido, Llave de (la)	Ignition, key
Enganche (el)	Hooking-up (for towing)
Escobilla (la)	Windscreen wiper
Escobilla/s (las)	Wiper (blade) Also brush.
Espejo (el): espejo retrovisor.	Mirror: Rear view mirror
Espejo lateral (el)	Wing mirror
Estárter (el)	Choke
Exéntrica (el)	Tappet
Faro Antiniebla (el)	Fog light
Faros (los)	Headlights
Filtro de aceite (el)	Oil filter
Filtro de aire (el)	Air Filter
Freno de mano (el)	Handbrake

Spanish	English
Freno / s (el) - Frenos de antibloqueo	Brake / s - ABS Brakes
Funda (de coche)	Cover (car)
Fundición (la)	Cast Iron (engine-block, etc).
Furgón *and* Furgoneta (la)	A **large van** and a small van.
Fusible (el)	Fuse
Fusibles (los)	Fuses
Gama (la)	Range (of choices)
Gamuza de piel (la)	Chamois leather
Garaje (el)	Garage (for parking?)
Gama (la)	Range (Range of models, etc.).
Gamuza de piel	Chamois leather
Gancho de remolque (el)	Tow bar.
Garaje (el)	Garage (for parking)
Gasoleo (el)	Diesel fuel.
Gasolinera	Petrol (Fuel) Station
Gasolina (la) (sin plomo)	Petrol. (unleaded).
Gato carretilla (el)	Jack, trolley.
Giro (el)	Turn (as in steering turning circle).
Glorieta	Roundabout or traffic circle.
Grua (la)	Breakdown truck
Guantes (los)	Gloves
Guardabarro (el)	Mudguard
Guarnición de freno	Brake lining

Spanish	English
Indicador de la gasoline/gasoleo (el)	Fuel gauge
Indicador de nivel de aceite (el)	Oil gauge
Injector	Injector
Intermitentes (las)	Turn indicators
Juego (de)	Set (of)
Junta (el)	Gasket
Lampara y faro (la) – (el)	Lamp & bulb
Lavaparabrisas	Glass cleaner. (for windscreen reservoir?)
Leva	Cam
Limpialuneta	Headlight washer
Limpiaparabrisas (los)	Windscreen wipers
Liquido de Frenos (el)	Brake fluid
Liquido de Servidireccion (el)	Power Steering oil
Liquido refrigerante (el)	Coolant (Engine)
Llantas de aleación (las)	Wheels, alloy.
Llave de contacto	Ignition key
Luz de freno (la)	Brake light
Luces de marchas atrás (las)	Reversing lights
Luces traseros (las)	Rear lights
Luz de advertencia (la)	Warning light
Maletero (el)	Boot (USA, - trunk)

Spanish	English
Mando/s (el)	Control/s
Manillar	Handlebar
Manómetro (el)	Gauge (pressure)
Manos (la) (libre)	Hands (free, as in mobile phone kit)
Manguera del radiador (arriba/abajo) (la)	Radiator hose (top/bottom)
Matrícula (la)	License Plate/Number
Mecánico (el) or mecánica: female.	Mechanic
Mezcla	Two-stroke petrol
Mitades	Split, as in folding rear seat on some cars.
Monovolúmen (Adj.)	People-carrier . (e.g. coche monovolumen)
Moto (la)	Motorcycle
Motor (el)	Engine
Motor de arranque (el)	Starter Motor
Muelle (el)	Spring (also pier or quay).
Neumático (el): Llanta (la)	Tyre: wheel rim
Ordenador (el)	Computer.
Palanca de cambios (la)	Gear selection lever
Pantalla (la)	Screen (TV , etc).
Parabrisos (el)	Windscreen
Parachoque (el) (delantero/trasera)	Bumper (front/rear)
Pastillos de frenos (los)	Brake pads
Pedal (el)	Pedal
Pedal (el)	Pedal (bicycle)
Pedal de freno.	Brake pedal

Spanish	English
Permiso de conducción	Driving licence
Peso (oficial) (el)	Weight (manufacturer's?)
Pie (el) *(Literally foot)*	Stand (support, motorcycle, etc).
Piel (la)	Skin & Leather
Piloto (el or la)	Driver
Pinchado (el)	Puncture
Pintura metalizada	Metallic paint.
Pistón	Piston
Potencia	Power, engine, eg, ? CV @ ? rpm
Presion (la)	Pressure
Presion de inflado	Tyre (inflation) pressure
Protector de la cadena (el)	Chainguard
Pulgada / os (la)	Inch / es (Used for wheel diameter)
Radiador (el)	Radiator
Radio (la)	Spoke (wheel)
Ranchera (el)	Estate car, station-wagon (US)
Recibo (el)	Receipt (for goods/services)
Rejilla (or colador)	Strainer (oil)
Remolque	Trailer, semi-trailer or caravan.
Rendimientos (el)	Performance (figures)
Resorte helice (el)	Spring, Coil
Respaldo de asiento (el)	Seat back
Retrovisor (el)	Driving mirror
Rin de la rueda (el)	Wheel rim

Spanish	English
Rotula ((la)	Ball & Socket joint
Rotunda (la)	Roundabout
Rueda de repuesta (la)	Spare wheel
Ruedas (las) delantera / trasera (s)	Wheels, front/rear
Salpicadero (el)	Dashboard
Seguro (el)	Lock
Seguro a todo riesgo	Comprehensive insurance
Servo freno	Brake servo
Silla (la)	Seat
Silenciador (el)	Silencer
Suspensión	Suspension
Taller (el)	Garage (for repairs)
Taller (el)	Workshop
Tambor de freno (el)	Brake drum
Tapacubos (el)	Hub caps/wheel trims
Tapicería (la)	Upholstery (seat covering, etc)
Tapa del depósito de gasolina/gasoleo (la)	Fuel tank **cap** or **flap**.
Techo solar (el)	Sun roof
Termostato	Thermostat
Testigo	Warning light
Timbre (el)	Bell
Tornillo (el)	Bolt, or screw
Todo terreno	4-wheel drive (all terrain)
Tracción (delantera o trasera)	Type of Drive (front or rear)
Traffic jam	Embotellamiento (el)
Transmisión (la)	Transmission

SPANISH	ENGLISH
Trasero, traseros	Rear (adjective)
Tratamiento	Treatment
Triángulos de emergencia	Emergency triangles
Tubo de escape (el)	Exhaust system
Turismo (el)	Saloon or passenger car
Valvula (la)	Valve (tyre, engine, etc)
Válvula de admisión	Inlet valve
Válvula de escape	Exhaust valve
Velocidad máximo	Maximum speed
Velocímetro (el)	Speedometer
Ventanilla (la)	Window
Ventana (la)	Window
Ventilador (el)	Fan
Visor (el)	Visor
Volante (el)	Steering wheel
Ventana (la)	Window
Ventilador (el)	Fan
Visor (el)	Visor
Volante (el)	Steering wheel
Accelerator	Acelarador (el)
ABS (brakes)	Antibloqueo
Air Filter	Filtro de aire (el)
Air/water	Aire/Agua
Air-con. drive belt	Correa del aircondicianado (la)

ENGLISH	SPANISH
Air-con. drive belt	Correa del aircondicianado (la)
Alignment (wheels)	Alineación
Alloy (wheels)	Aleación (de ruedas)
Alternator	Alternador (el)
Antifreeze.	Anticongelante (el)
Anti-theft.	Antirobbo.
Automatic gearbox.	Cambio automática
Axle (wheel)	Eje (de rueda) (el)
Balance weight (wheel)	Contrapeso
Ball & Socket joint	Rotula (la)
Battery	Bateria (la)
Battery charger.	Cargador de bateria
Bearing. (ball) (roller)	Cojinete (el) (de bolas) (de rodillos).
Bell.	Timbre (el)
Belt, drive, (toothed) for cylinder-head valves.	Correa de la distribución. (la)
Block (engine) and **head** (cylinder).	Bloque y Culata.
Bodywork.	Carrocería.
Bonnet or Hood (USA).	Capó (el)
Boot or Trunk (USA).	Maletero (el)
Bore and stroke, cylinder.	Cotas (las) In specifications!
Brake/s.	Freno/s. (los)
Brake disk.	Disco de freno. (el)
Brake drum.	Tambor de freno. (el)
Brake fluid.	Liquido de Freno. (el)
Brake light.	Luz de freno. (la)

English	Spanish
Brake lining	Guarnición de freno
Brake pads	Pastillos de frenos (los)
Brake pedal (clutch)	Pedal de freno (el) (de embrague)
Brake servo	Servo freno (el)
Breakdown	Averia (la)
Breakdown truck	Grua (la)
Bumper	Parachoque (el)
Cable	Cable (el)
Cam	Leva (la)
Cam cover	Culato (el)
Camshaft	Arbol de levas (el)
Car	Coche (el)
Caravan	Caravana (la)
Cargador CD (la)	CD changer
Car park	Aparcamiento (el)
Carburettor	Carburador (el)
Cast iron, of (engine block, etc).	Fundición, de
Catalytic Converter	Catalizador (el)
CD Changer	Cargador CD
Central locking	Cierre centrolizado (el)
Chain	Cadena (la)
Chainguard.	Protector de la cadena (el)
Chains for snow	Cadenas para la nieve
Chamois leather	Gamuza de piel (la)
Chassis	Bastidor (el)
Choke	Estárter (el)
Clock.	Reloj (el)
Clutch.	Embrague (el)

English	Spanish
Coil Ignition	Bobina (la)
Comprehensive insurance	Seguro a todo riesgo
Connecting rod (engine)	Biela (bieletta, suspension?) (la)
Coolant (Engine)	Liquido refrigerante del motor (el)
Control/s	Mando/s (el)
Cover (car)	Funda (de coche)
Crankshaft	Cigüeñal (el)
Crash-helmet	Casco (el)
Dashboard	Salpicadero (el)
Diesel fuel	Gasoleo (el)
Distributor	Distribuidor (el)
Driver	Piloto (Feminine, pilota)
Driving licence	Permiso de conducción. (el)
Driving mirror	Retrovisor (el)
Drive-shaft	Arbol de transmisión (el)
Emergency triangles	Triángulos de emergencia (los)
Engine	Motor (el)
Engine capacity	Cilindrada
Exhaust system	Tubo de escape (el)
Exhaust-valve	Válvula de escape.
Fan	Ventilador (el)
Fan-belt	Correa del ventilador (la)
Finish	Acabado
Fog light	Faro anti-niebla (el)
Four-stroke	Cuatro tiempo
Frame	Cuadro (el)
Front (adjective)	Delantara

English	Spanish
Fuel 95 or 98 octane non-lead 97 Lead replacement petrol. Diesel (1st quality)	Combustible 95 or 98 Sin plomo gasolina. 97 gasolina Gasoleo or diesel
Fuel Consumption (average).	Consumo medio or mixto.
Fuel gauge	Indicador de la gasoline/gasoleo (el)
Fuel system	Alimentación (la)
Fuel tank	Depòsito del combustible. (el)
Fuel tank **cap** or **flap**.	**Tapa** del depósito de gasoline/gasoleo (la)
Fuse, Fuses	Fusible (el) Fusibles (los)
Garage (for parking or at home)	Garaje (el)
Garage (for repairs, workshop)	Taller (el)
Gasket	Junta (el)
Gauge (pressure)	Manómetro (el)
Gear selection lever	Palanca de cambios (la)
Gearbox	Caja de cambios (la)
Glass cleaner. (for windscreen reservoir?)	Lava parabrisos
Gloves	Guantes (los)
Hand (-free kit) For mobile phones.	(kit) manos de libres
Handbrake	Freno de mano (el)
Handlebar (Bike & Motorcycle, etc.).	Manillar
Handbrake	Freno de mano (el)
Handlebar (Bike & Motorcycle, etc.).	Manillar
Headlights	Faros (los)
Heater	Calentador (el)
Helmet, motorcycle.	Casco (el) de moto
Horn	Bocina or Pito or Klaxon (el)
Hub caps/wheel trims	Tapa cubos

English	Spanish
Ignition key	Llave de contacto o Encendido, (la)
Inch (used for wheel diameter)	Pulgada (la)
Injector	Injector
Inlet valve	Válvula de admisión
Inner Tube	Camara (la)
Insurance	Seguro
Jack, trolley.	Gato carretilla (el)
Key	Llave (la) Say "lee-ar-vey"
Lamp & bulb	Lamparo y faro (la) – (el)
Leather	Cuero (el)
License Plate/Number	Matrícula (la) (or placa)
Lock	Seguro (el) or cerradura
Maximum Speed	Velocidad máximo
Mechanic	Mecánico (el) or mecánica: female.
Metallic paint.	Pintura metalizada.
Mirror	Espejo ((el)
Moped	Ciclomoto ((el)
Motorcycle	Moto (la)
Mountain bike	Bicicleta de montaña (la)
Mudguard	Guardabarro (el)
Odometer	Cuentakilómetras (el)
Oil, Oil-can.	Aceite (el) Acietera (la)
Oil filter.	Filtro de aceite (el)
Oil gauge	Indicador de nivel de aceite (el)
Panel beater	Carrocero / a (el or la)
Panel beater / body shop, also..	Chapa y Pintura. (sign outside)
People carrier	Coche monovolúmen.
Pedal (foot, also bicycle)	Pedal (el)
Performance	Rendimiento / s (el / los)
Petrol	Gasolino (la)

English	Spanish
Petrol (Fuel) Station	Gasolinera
Piston	Pistón
Power, Engine.	Potencia
Power-steering	Dirección asistida (la)
Power Steer drive belt	Correa del servodireccion (la)
Power Steering oil	Liquido de Servidireccion (el)
Pressure	Presion (la)
Pump	Bomba (la)
Puncture	Pinchado (el)
Rack and Pinion (Steering?)	Cremallera y piñón.
Radiator	Radiador (el)
Radiator hose (top/bottom)	Manquera del radiador (arriba/abajo) (la)
Range (of choices)	Gama (la)
Rear (adjective)	Trasero
Rear lights	Luces traseros (las)
Receipt (for goods/services)	Recibo (el)
Reflector (auto)	Catafaras (el)
Reservoir	Deposito de liquido
Reversing lights	Luces de marchas atrás (las)
Roof rack.	Baca (la)
Roundabout	Glorieta and rotunda (both "la")
Saloon (or passenger) car	Turismo (el)
Screen (TV or navigation)	Pantalla. (la)
Screw, or bolt	Tornillo (el)
Seat front/rear	Asiento or silla delantro/trasero
Seat back	Respaldo de asiento. (el)
Seat belt	Cinturón de seguridad (el)
Set (of)	Juego (de)
Shock absorbers	Amortiguadores (los)
Silencer	Silenciador (el)
Spare wheel	Rueda de repuesta (la)
Spark plug	Bujía (la)

English	Spanish
Speaker (radio)	Altavoz
Speedometer	Velocímetro (el)
Speed trap	Control de velocidad
Spoke (wheel)	Radio (la)
Sports car	Deportivo
Spring, general.	Muelle (el)
Spring, Coil	Resorte helice (el)
Stand (support, motorcycle, etc).	Pie (el) *(Literally foot)*
Starter Motor	Motor de arranque (el)
Steering	Dirección
Steering column	Columna de dirección (el)
Steering wheel	Volante (el)
Strainer (oil)	Rejilla
Sump (Oil, bottom of engine)	Cárter
Sun roof	Techo solar (el)
Suspension	Suspensión
Tappet	Exéntrica (el)
Thermostat	Termostato
Tow bar	Ganch de remolque (el)
Traffic jam.	Embotellamiento (el)
Trailer	Remolque
Transmission	Transmisión (la)
Treatment	Tratamiento
Truck, Truck Driver	Camión (el) Camiónero
Turn, turning distance (steering)	Giro (el)
Turn indicators	Intermitentes (las)
Two-stroke	Dos tiempo

English	Spanish
Two-stroke petrol	Mezcla
Tyre (inflation) pressure	Presion de inflato
Tyre: Wheel rim	Neumático (el): la Llanta
Upholstery	Tapicería (la)
Valve (tyre, engine, etc)	Valvula (la)
Van / wagon.	Furgón (el) or furgoneta (smaller-van) (la)
Visor	Visor (el)
Warning light	Luz de advertencia (la)
Warning light	Testigo
Water bottle	Botella para el agua (la)
Wheel rim	Rin de la rueda (el)
Wheel trim. (Plastic clip on?)	Tapàcubo (el)
Wheel - front/rear	Rueda (la) delantera/trasera
Wheel, steel.	Llanta de acero (la)
Wheels, alloy.	Llantas de aleación (las)
Window	Ventana (la)
Windows, electric .	Elevalunas eléctrico (los)
Windscreen	Parabrisos (el)
Windscreen wiper.	Escobilla (la)
Windscreen wipers.	Limpiaparabrisas or escobillos (los)
Wing mirror.	Espejo lateral (el)
Workshop.	Taller (el)

PART 8-2

ENGLISH TO SPANISH PHRASES USEFUL ON THE ROAD.

The following phrases can be used to ensure that the Spanish speaker supplying a service, etc., can quickly understand what you need.

At the Service Station (Fuel)/*Gasolinera.*

English	Spanish	Phonetic Pronunciation
Fill it up, please	Lleno, por favor.	Lee-en-o, por fabor.
(?) litres of petrol/diesel	(?) litros de gasolina / diesel, por favor.	(¿) litros deh gasoleena/deesel por fabor.
95 non-lead: 98 non lead super: 97 (leaded petrol) Diesel.	95 sin plomo: 98 sin plomo súper: 97 con plomo: Gasóleo o Diesel.	95 seen plomo 98 seen plomo sooper 97 con plomo Gasóleeo or Deesel
Where is the air and water?	¿Dónde esta el aire y agua?	Dondeh esta el ayreh ee agwa
Where is the next service station?	¿Dónde esta la próxima gasolinera?	Dondeh esta la prokseema gasoleenera

Parking/*aparcimiento.*

Is there a car park nearby?	¿Hay un aparcamiento cerca?	Eye oon aparkameeyento terca?
Do you have some change for the parking meter?	¿Tienen cambio para el parquímetro?	Teeyenen kambeeyo para el parkeemetro
My car has been clamped Who do I call?	A mi coche le han puesto el cepo. ¿A quien llamo?	A mee coche leh an pwesto el thepo. A keeyen l-yamo.
What is the charge per hour/day/week?	¿Cuánto cobran por hora / dia / semana?	Kwanto kobran por ora/deeya/cemana

Breakdown/*Averiarse.*

I have had a breakdown.	He tenido una avería	Eh teneedoh oona abereeya
Can you send a mechanic/ breakdown truck?	¿Puede mandar a un mecánico / una grúa?	Puede mandar a oon mekaneeko / oona groowa
I belong to (?) rescue service.	Soy del servicio de grúa (?)	Soy del serbeetheeyo del groowa ...
Where is the nearest garage?	¿Dónde esta el taller más cercano?	Dondeh esta el tal-yer mas therkano
The car is a (make and colour) on the (road) near (km signpost or identifying sign)	El coche esta en (...) en la (.. autopista, etc) cerca (...)Or .. kilómetros de (SOS post, etc?).	El coche esta en la auto-peesta cerca...Or .. kilómetros deh ....
How long will you be?	¿Cuánto tiempo tardado?	Kwanto teeyempo tardara
I do not know what is wrong.	No se que le pasa	No seh kay le pasa.
I have locked the keys in the car.	Me ha dejado las llaves en le coche.	Meh eh dekhado las l-yabes en el kocheh.

Accidents. (Tel. 112, Emergency).

In the event of an accident, if you are able, remember to place two triangles facing the traffic, one about 100 metres/yards away and the other about 10-20 metres/yards away, both facing the oncoming traffic. If the road is very narrow and two-way, place one facing the traffic behind about 75 to 100 metres away, and one on the opposite side of the road at a similar distance for safety. Give plenty of distance warning to allow adequate safe braking for the other traffic.

You must always report to the local police if someone is injured, and you should if there is an insurance claim. Do it later if no one is injured. Fill in an accident report. Obtain the **police report number** from the police station. Show your driver's licence and insurance (green) card: complete an insurance accident form with the other driver if possible and get his/her signature. **Do not admit to any fault** regardless of what happened, and do not sign a statement other than the insurance report **if you agree with it (**or your lawyer agrees later). Note the safety condition of the other vehicle including tyres and for evidence of drink or drugs used by the other driver.

There has been an accident!	Ha habido un accidente	A abeedo oon actheedente
Can you help me please?	¿Puede ayudarme, por favor?	Puede ayoodarmeh, por fabor
It is ..... (location)	Ha ocurrido	A okooreedo
.. on the motorway	En la autopista	En la aootopeesta
.. on the bypass (around or through a town.	.. en la carretera	En la carreterra
Near	Cerca de	Therca deh
Where is the nearest telephone? (SOS on autopista)	¿Dónde está el teléfono más cercano / SOS?	Dondeh esta el telefono mas therkano
Call	Llame a	Le-ameh a
... the police	La policia	La poleethia
... ambulance	Una ambulancia	Oona amboolantheea
... a doctor	Un medico	Oon medeeko
... the fire brigade	El cuerpo del bomberos	El kwerpo deh bomberos
There are people injured.	Hay gente herida	Eye khente hereda
He / she is seriously injured.	Esta gravemente herido/a	Esta grabamenteh ereedo/a
He / she is unconscious.	Esta sangrando / a	Esta sangrando/a
Do not move him/her.	No le mueva	No le mueva

Repairs.

Do you do repairs?	¿Hacen reparaciones?	athen reparatheeyones
The (part) is not working	El / la (part) no funciona	El/la ... no funchiona
Can you repair it? (temporarily)	¿Puede hacerle una reparación? (provisional)	Puede atherle oona reparatheeyon? (probeeseeyanol).
Please make only essential repairs.	Por favor, hágale reparaciones básicas solamente	Por fabor, hágale reparatheeyones baseekas solomentah

Can I wait for it?	¿Puedo espera?	Pwedeh esperar
Can you repair it for today?	¿Puede arreglarlo hoy?	Puede arreglarlo oy
When will it be ready?	¿Cuándo estará listo?	Kwando estara leesto
How much?	¿El cuánto?	El kwanto
That is too expensive!	¡Es muy, muy caro!	Es moy moy karo
May I have the receipt (for my insurance), please?	Pueden darme un recibo (para el seguro), por favor?	Pueden darme un retheebo (para el segooro) por fabor.

Possible Answers. Show the Spanish mechanic this table.

No tenga las piezas necesarias.	I do not have the parts needed.
Solo pueda reparo provisionalmente.	I can only do a temporary repair.
Tendré que mandar a pedir las piezas.	I will have to order the parts.
Mas o menos, … horas / días / semanas.	More or less ..... Hours/days/weeks.
Su coche / camino no tiene arreglo.	Your car / truck is not repairable.
Estará listo (tiempo y fecha).	It will be ready (time and date). Ask mechanic to write details.
Hoy mismo.	Later today.
A la mañana.	Tomorrow.

Insurance Matters.

I would like an interpreter, please.	Quiero un interprete, por favor.	Keeyero unn eenterpreteh, por fabor.
What is your name and address?	¿Cuál es su nombre y su dirección?	Kwal es soo nombrey ee soo deereektheeyon
Your insurance, please.	Su seguro, por favor.	Soo segooro, por fabor
The car / motorcycle ran into me!	El coche / moto choco conmigo	El kochey / moto choko konmeego
He / she saw it happen.	El / ella lo vio	El / e-yah lo beeyo

I had right of way!	¡Yo tenia derecha de paso!	Yo teneeya derecho deh paso
(He / she) was driving too fast!	¡Conducía demasiado / a rápida!	Condoothia demasiado/a rapeedo
(He / she) was driving too close!	¡Conducía demasiado / a cerca!	Condoothia demasiado/a terca

Show the other (Spanish) driver, etc. to see what is needed.

¿Puedo ver su ..., por favor.?.... (1) permiso de conducir... (2) certificado del seguro... (3) documento del regristo o "permiso de circulación" del vehículo.	Can I see your .... , please? ...(1) driver's licence. ...(2) insurance card/certificate. ...(3) vehicle registration papers.
¿A que hora ocurrió?	When did it happen?
¿Dónde ocurrió?	Where did it happen?
¿Hubo alguien más involucrado?	Was anyone else involved?
¿Hay testigos?	Any witnesses?
¿Se paso el limite de velocidad?	Were you speeding?
¡Sus faros no funcionan!	Your lights are not working (or on)!
¡Tendrá que pagar una multa!	You will have to pay a fine (on the spot).
Tenemos que tomar su declaración en la comisaría.	You will have to make a statement the police station
¿Por favor, una grúa?	Please call a breakdown truck?

PART 9-1

VEHICLE DRIVER INSURANCE NEEDS IN SPAIN.

Driving in Spain is a pleasant experience, -- except in the rush hours in the major cities, where the old and narrow roads and the volume of traffic means that public transport (or "shank's pony) is to be preferred especially at holiday times. The country roads are relatively empty and the majority of Spanish drivers polite and courteous. The author has driven from Madrid to Malaga on the main road in early June, in mid-week, and been pleasantly surprised at the very low volume of traffic on that major trunk road. However, in the holiday areas especially in July and August, the roads (and beaches) are crowded with holiday-makers, Spanish as well as other Europeans, etc., and then driving is no pleasure, - and can be dangerous.

A French vehicle can often be identified by the large amount of luggage on the roof.

As elsewhere in the civilised world insurance is a legal requirement, as it should be to protect all of us road users, and driving without it carries severe penalties. Reports in the Spanish Press indicate that as many as **25% of moped/scooter riders** do not have insurance, possibly due to the relative high cost because of the low ages of most riders, and the generally reckless driving habits of many in this group. There are quite a few motorcar drivers without insurance due to cost and their low income, it is therefore doubly important that if involved in an accident with particularly one of these road users, especially where they are injured, you obtain all details (refer to the **accident report form** in this book) and also obtain the names of any reliable witnesses, which is not always easy due to language differences. If you have a mobile phone contact the *Guardia Civil* or *Policia Nacional* if on the open road, and the **Policia Local** if in a town, and you must do if someone is hurt. All can be contacted through one number, **112, the equivalent of 999 in the UK, and 911 in the USA**. Usually, someone will speak English, and if someone is injured you must do this as instructed by Spanish Law.

Spain, whether you are at fault or not, if someone is hurt, you should always rely on a local lawyer to represent you to avoid any possible later charges and claims by the other driver. Your insurance covers these costs only up to a limit, so **please check your policy** and take advice. Also, the insurance company's lawyer works for them, not you.

AS A VISITOR TO SPAIN.

Check that your insurance covers you fully in the countries you are to drive in, and you must carry your policy certificate (used to be called the green card) with the information showing this. It is also advisable to discuss with your insurance company extra public liability insurance as, if **you are judged at fault** in an accident and the other party / ies, or your passengers (but not those relatives) or pedestrians, etc., are injured and/or property damaged, the Criminal Court, can, and often does, set the amount of damages to be paid by the guilty party. It is important that you have **adequate liability cover**. No civil claim needs to be made at a later date, unless the other party considers that the damages were not enough, so it is very important to be represented by your **own lawyer**. Any fines and damages usually have to be paid immediately, and if insured, this is not a problem (except when your next premium is due). If you are not insured, the Court may take action to ensure you cannot leave Spain without positive guarantees of payment. This can include imprisonment and / or impounding of your goods, usually the vehicle unless it is not worth enough. The current law specifies for all drivers in Spain that they must have public liability for third-party **body injuries** of up to Eur.337.000 and for **damages to other property,** including walls, etc., just over Eur.96.000. In practice, you are advised to ensure cover for much more to avoid personal liability from your own assets, for example, Eur.1.000.000 and Eur.250.000. This extra cover is not usually that much more expensive. Please note that "bodily injury" claims do not normally include **members of your own family**, but can include other passengers.

It is also a good idea to have a **bail bond facility** so you do not spend "weeks" in jail because you cannot afford the set bail. Your insurance agent will advise you on this facility if you are not familiar with it.

Another important point is that the insurance companies will usually pay only from **Eur.3.000 to Eur.6.000** for your defence **legal fees** (check your policy), and remember that they are

working for the insurance company, not for you, and their main task is to protect the company. Extra separate insurance may be a good idea here for this reason. The insurance company usually appoints their lawyer, and gives you no choice of yours.

It is worth remembering that in Spain, the "consortium of insurance companies" pays out Third Party damages on behalf of uninsured drivers, **using the specified lower limits above**, so it is worth ensuring that your and your family's own personal injury and liability insurance provides adequate cover for your <u>own sakes</u> as well as other parties. I am sure you will agree that any driver **not insured at all** should be considered a "parasite" by all road-users, as the insured's premiums often pay for the actions of the uninsured where it is impossible or impracticable to recover the costs from the uninsured. A recent report in the UK stated that the insurance companies charge 30 per policy issued to cover damages caused by uninsured drivers there.

INSURING A MOTOR VEHICLE IN SPAIN.

As in all European countries, there are basically three types of cover: Third Party only (*tercero solo*), Third Party Fire and Theft (*tercero, contra incedios y robo*), and Fully Comprehensive (*total riesgo*), and the minimum insurance is Third Party. All insurance must include the minimum public liability as advised in the paragraph above. Many companies in Spain will not issue Comprehensive, or even Fire and Theft cover for older cars, say ten years plus. Your broker will advise, and good ones have their policies and other important information in English to give to you.

You may insure a foreign plated car here but not with a Spanish company based in Spain (the broker may have an arrangement with a company in say Gibraltar), or even from outside the EU. If you have problems in Spain, try the companies in Gibraltar. Most companies photograph the car if it is not new to prevent early false damage claims, -- such are the morals of some people. They will also check and report on the car's condition visually.

If you have a UK registered car here "permanently", and drive it back to the UK occasionally, remember that it must have passed the UK- MOT to be legal there, and should have the UK, etc. road tax paid. The police know how to check the discs. (See in s book for more information on foreign plated cars in Spain, part 4-2). No Claims scounts / bonuses can be as much as 50% (or more: the author's is 60%), especially if you e over 55 years of age with maximum no-claims bonuses, and of good health. It is therefore portant to ensure that you keep this bonus by making sure that you are not to blame in an cident, even by false information from the other driver.

e only supply the basic advice here, as there are insurance brokers and companies who can swer every detailed query.

THE EVENT OF AN ACCIDENT.

 in any EU (or most others) country, it is vital that, where possible, you follow a procedure er an accident. The following applies: -

ay calm and be polite, even if the other driver is angry. If you do not speak Spanish and the ner driver does not speak English, say, "*No hablo Español*" (no ablo espanyol). (There is, of urse, also the chance that the other driver may be German or French, etc., and this is where e pertinent phrase book is useful). **Never admit that you are at fault**. Your insurance licy instructions usually specify this and your cover could be affected **if you admit fault**. ere are some useful phrase translations **in Part 8 – 2.**

someone is injured, the police **must be called**, as well as an ambulance. **Telephone 112**, e equivalent Spanish emergency number for the **UK's - 999** or **USA's – 911** numbers. On e Malaga coast, some policemen speak a little, or better, English, and they are very helpful, unless you are abusive or drunk, of course. If they suspect you have been drinking or you e under the influence of some substance, the police may ask for a drug and alcohol test to taken, and the penalty for refusal is often more than if you fail the test, plus a sizable fine r "civil disobedience".

se the special accident report form issued by your insurance company, if a rental car, there ll be one in the glove compartment. If not, use a copy of the English one (photocopy it?) in is book, or use the other driver's form translating the headings with your copy. The form is cceptable to any insurance company (in the EU) whether it is Spanish, English, German, etc. hat is why it is the same layout in all languages. This form is called the *Declaración amistosa de accidente de automóvil,* or "Agreed statement of facts on motor vehicle accident", and if you do not have one, either get one from your broker or photocopy the one in this book (three copies) and carry them with you, with carbon paper, to either complete or to use with the other driver's form's Spanish headings at the accident scene. The other driver from an EU country may have his form in French, if he/she is from France, but the form may be completed in two languages, as long as it is **agreed to be correct** and is **signed by both drivers**. Exchange copies of the report forms. They are in three parts, one for the insurance company, one for you, and one for the other driver. It is worth remembering that the contents of the form are **legally binding in Court if signed by both drivers**.

They **must not be altered** once completed and signed. To do so renders them inadmissible, and the driver concerned may suffer a penalty with the insurance company.

It is suggested that you familiarise yourself with all the forms and procedure occasionally. Make sure you are familiar with **all paper work** before setting out on your journey to or in Spain. Do not sign the other driver's accident form if you are not **absolutely sure it is correct** (language?), and remember to get a copy of it for your insurer (and lawyer, if applicable).

Keep a black, fine point ballpoint pen in the car for completing the form. It is also always a good idea too have a camera in the car. The "throwaway" ones are OK for this purpose.

It is important to record the other driver's name, driver's licence number and place of issue, street home address, phone number and vehicle registration of the other driver, if possible, checked by reference to the vehicles official papers that must be kept in the glove compartments in all vehicles in Spain, as opposed to just verbal advice.

If the other driver/s is a foreigner, obtain passport number and place of issue, **OR** if they are resident in Spain, their *residencia* card / paper number (**NIF** or **NIE**) and (Spanish? – with their address in it) Driving Licence details. You should also check the vehicle VIN number if it is a "late" model car. This is in the dash on the LH side and can be seen through the windscreen. Do not panic if the other driver is **not insured** as the consortium of insurance companies in Spain will pay out to a certain degree if the other driver is Spanish and not insured and is at fault, but be even more careful about getting the correct details, and phone the police to attend (Tel. 112). If you are suspicious, take a photo of the driver if you can.

Obtain all details of witness / es, especially if you know you are not at fault.

Get the names and numbers of the police officers present.

If you have a **camera with you**, take pictures of the vehicles' damages and accident area, including skid marks and **measure important dimensions** (paces will do) before the vehicles are moved if possible. This action could greatly help your case especially if you are not at fault. If you are not able to do so at the time of the accident, come back at a later time to measure and take photos.

DO NOT MAKE ANY ALTERATIONS ON THE ACCIDENT FORM AFTER IT HAS BEEN SIGNED AND CARBON COPIES SEPARATED. SEND IT TO YOUR INSURER ASAP.

Check quickly to see if the other vehicle is un-roadworthy in anyway, e. g. worn tyres, windscreen excessively dirty, wipers not working properly if raining, driver tired or been drinking or on drugs (pupils dilated?), vehicle overloaded, etc. Please note that if there is such a fault, their insurance company will usually pay you out, but claim from the other driver, as they would with you if you were unfit to drive. Remember that drivers are not insured if their vehicle is not roadworthy or they are unfit to drive, but if he/she is at fault, you will still get paid.

If you wish to make an official criminal charge (*denuncia*) for the other driver's dangerous driving, etc., you have **up to two months** to do so at the local police station (*Policia Local* or *Municipal*).

Use a local lawyer (*abogado*) who is a specialist in these matters and especially one **fluent in your language.** If a **visitor to Spain**, check with your own insurance company first for preferred representatives in Spain, but if none are forthcoming, obtain reliably recommended local lawyer's details. It is also advantageous if **they** have E-mail as a communication method as this is by far the most reliable and inexpensive way today, especially if you are back in your own country. Many still only use fax machines.

If resident in Spain, your insurance company can handle the legal details, and most have arrangements with companies in other EU countries for such work.

If possible, ensure that the car is taken to a reputable panel-beater / repair shop recommended by your insurance company if possible, who will be expecting to be advised of the accident within the time as stated in the policy anyway. Ask them as soon as possible about the recommended repair shop as delays may occur otherwise. Remove all valuables and loose items, and avoid "hole in wall businesses". If you are not sure, take it to the local **official dealer** for your vehicle who will handle the repair for you and deal with your insurance company.

If the damage is to your vehicle is minimal, consider paying for the repair yourself to speed the repair time and eliminate a claim, which is covered only by your insurance excess.   You should **still advise your company** though, as specified in the policy to avoid future problems, but stress that it is "**not a claim**" to keep your NCB.

Litigation can take a long time, but it works, although at time of printing, a new criminal (as opposed to civil) system has been introduced called "fast trials" (*Juicios Rapidos*) which can result in a verdict within a very short time (24 hours?).   If a you are a visitor, it is stressed again that it is important to have a local specialist lawyer who could save you wasted trips coming to Spain in the event of a Court case, and if you appoint one remember to sign a **Power of Attorney** so he / she can represent you without having to constantly contact you for instructions while you are in your home country.

Your insurance company will normally pay for this.

PART 10-1

BUYING A VEHICLE IN SPAIN.

Buying a vehicle in Spain is useful if you have a holiday or have property here. You can bring your UK vehicle here whether or not you are resident, but eventually you will have to put it on Spanish plates if you wish to use it here full-time, although it is recommended to buy a left-hand drive vehicle.

Motorcycles are not a problem as far as the driving position is concerned, but the main differences with cars from the UK are: -

1. The obvious one is that the steering wheel is on the opposite side of the car to those in mainland Europe. This is **not a problem for good drivers** who maintain a fair distance from the vehicle in front and overtake correctly (as advised by the Institute of Advanced Motorists and all good driving schools). When you are on your own and need to collect/pay for parking or at toll road cash booth, you need to be able to easily stretch over the front passenger seat or you will have to get out.

2. If you intend to keep the car in Spain for more than six months and use it as well, you will have to transfer it to Spanish registration plates. If you only use it for the allowed six months, you will still have to go back to the country of origin to have it safety tested, and annually pay any road-taxes, which are often more expensive than Spain's equivalent. You are not allowed officially to drive it in Spain for more that six months per year, but the author has evidence where the police (*Guardia Civil*?) have issued fines for the use of a foreign plated car for **only one month**, where they can **prove that you have taken up residence here.** You can avoid this by obtaining a Spanish police certificate stating that you are not resident here, as well as current receipts for water and electricity to show that you have a home **outside** of Spain, and the car is used to travel back and forth. Use a *gestor* if your Spanish is not good.

3. If you wish to sell the car in Spain, unless it is on Spanish plates or it is a sought after classic, you may have difficulties unless you can find someone who is moving back to UK, or the selling price will be much lower unless it is a valued classic.

4.   If the vehicle is from outside the EU, there are various technical specifications to which it must conform (EU homolgamation) to before it will be accepted for Spanish plates. This can cost you more money if the car does not conform.

It is better to buy a car in Spain if you intend to stay, as it is difficult and costly to change a foreign non-EU car to Spanish plates.

BUYING A NEW OR USED CAR/MOTOR CYCLE IN SPAIN.

You are settled here for a while or "for ever" and need a new or used car, this is no problem as long as you have the following: -

1)   The necessary cash or credit facilities.

2)   You are registered as a resident with your local town hall (*Ayuntimiento,* the certificate called the *Nota de Empadronamiento*).

3)   You have an NIE (six-month form) or *residencia* ("permanent" – 2 / 5 year residency card).

4)   A copy of the *escritura* or property deed for your owned Spanish accommodation, **or** a current rental contract for at least one year. You will need this to get the *Nota de Empadronamiento.*

5)   You will need good photocopies as well as the originals of the above and your passport.

The same applies as anywhere else.   If your Spanish is not so good, you have two choices: pay someone to go to the dealer / seller to help you negotiate, or use a sales outlet where the people speak English. There are many of these in the holiday areas.

In both cases, you can do what the author did. Car sales were slow in July 2001, and the author (and his wife) decided to buy a new car after the accident to their BMW.   The local dealers have a maker's "corporate image" quotation form with the base car cost and then the options where the prices are inserted, the total being complete with local registration tax and the year's (or part of the year) road tax.   Now the first line of the quotation form is **the discount**, and this often depends on what the manufacturer states to the Dealer the discount for that model for that month and **is the same** at all the big car dealers.

The author took the quotation form to two other main dealers, both of whom had the same maker's discount) and obtained further substantial discount quotations in writing (same form). As a result, the car was bought at the English-speaking dealer at much less than the original price quoted.

Buying a used car is fraught with pitfalls if you are not fluent in Spanish. The Spanish people are nice to know but many seem to think that all foreigners are wealthy, so it is easier to buy from someone again who speaks English fluently if you do not have a good friend who can negotiate for you in Spanish. Used cars in good condition hold their values much more than in the UK at this time.

There are possibly three sources you can buy from.

1.   A **MAIN DEALER** for the make of car and model you want. They may also have a demonstrator model that you can buy for a good price, or one that has been traded in from a regular customer who has bought a new one. If the car is low mileage as it should be as a demonstrator model, the dealer may give you up to a year's warranty in writing (in Spanish) on it, but have the terms (to be legal, in Spanish) checked by an expert if it is not the manufacturer's standard warranty. Some manufacturers also have an extended warranty that may be transferred. Note that the standard new vehicle warranty in all the EU is now **two years** anyway.

2.   From a **PRIVATE SOURCE**. If you are experienced, and can check the car yourself, go ahead, but be careful as *caveat emptor* (let buyer beware) applies here. You can have the car checked by an expert at a reasonable cost.

3.   From a **CAR RENTAL COMPANY**. Official figures state that 6% of the cars registered in Spain are to rental companies. Spain has many rental agencies that sell off their cars from when they are one year-old to four year's-old, from when the technical inspection is due. As this market is fairly glutted, you can negotiate a good deal with a warranty, e.g. 3 months, to cover any serious problems. These cars are not as bad as you may think, depending on the company selling the car,

on the company selling the car, but do ask for copies of the servicing records to be shown on the spot so they are not made up ready for you later. A used rental car can be obtained for a good price, as little as 50% or more of the new price if three years plus old. If you are not mechanically minded, get the car checked by an independent engineer such as the *Real Automóvil Club de España (RACE—*pronounced "raathay".*)*, similar to RAC in the UK. Tel. 902 40 45 45: **www.race.net.club**. As it is a rental car, the owner will either rent it to you for a few days, or let you use it on test for free if you are a "good negotiator".

TRANSFER OF YOUR NEW PURCHASE.

There are formalities to follow and the dealer or car rental agency will normally carry out these on your behalf. If it is coming up for, or is more than four years old (five for *motos*), they will also have it tested for you (*ITV* or MOT). If not, make it part of the purchase deal, as it will save you much time, money and searching for the test station where English is not usually spoken. Do not rely on the testing procedure as being a sign that the car is in good condition. The author has seen old cars that have just been passed, with the front wheels ready to fall off due to serious suspension wear.

IT IS STRONGLY RECOMMENDED THAT YOU USE THE SERVICES OF A REPUTABLE *GESTOR* (LEGAL ADVISOR).

PART 10-2

SELLING YOUR VEHICLE IN SPAIN

When you sell your car/motorcycle, you can easily carry out the necessary paperwork yourself if your Spanish is up to it, or use the services of a *gestor*, or, if to a **reputable dealer**, they will do the work for you if you include it in the deal. Or a friend who is fluent.

IT IS VERY IMPORTANT TO ENSURE THAT THIS PROCEDURE IS COMPLETED CORRECTLY. IF IT IS NOT, DUE TO THERE BEING A TRANSFER TAX DUE WHICH IS NORMALLY PAID BY THE BUYER, BUT IS THE RESPONSIBILITY OF THE SELLER TO SEE THAT IT IS PAID. THEY GET YOU ALL WAYS! MANY BUYERS WILL AVOID THIS TAX IF POSSIBLE BY NOT TRANSFERRING THE VEHICLE. THIS MEANS THAT NOT ONLY ARE YOU THEN LIABLE TO A FINE <u>AND</u> THE TAX, BUT ANY TRAFFIC VIOLATIONS COMMITTED BY THE NEW OWNER CAN BE CHARGED TO YOU AS THE REGISTERED OWNER.

If you do it yourself, the following procedure applies: -

⇒ Go to the local Motor Vehicles Dept. (*Jefatura de Tráfico*) in your Province to obtain the necessary forms.

⇒ Make sure you have personal identification with you at all times.

⇒ You will need an **application form** (*notificacion de transferencia de vehiculos*). Complete in duplicate, one copy for the buyer, one copy for the *trafico* office.

⇒ The paid-up municipal vehicle tax **receipt** (Part 6—5), along with a photocopy.

⇒ Receipt for payment of the vehicle transfer tax, which is charged at **4%** on the sale of second-hand vehicles, based on the authority's tax tables. This tax is paid to the local tax (*hacienda*) office, and is called the *impuesto sobre transmisiones patrimonales y actos juridicos documentados, or* ITP in short. They have a list of values of all vehicles so they will set the actual amount to which the percentage for the tax is applied, which reduces each year until the car is ten years old, and then it is set at 10% of the **original value**. The 4% tax is based on this value and is normally **paid by the buyer,** although it is the **responsibility of the seller** to see it is paid. The tax is declared on *Forma 620, compra/venta de vehiculos usados*

137

entre particulares, which, like most legal forms in Spain, may be bought at any **tobacconists or *estancos*,** or the tax office *(hacienda)*, and the tax must be paid within 30 days of transfering the vehicle.

⇒ If applicable, a current ITV (mechanical fitness test) report (if the car is over four years old) with photocopy. This report is the *Inspeccion Tecnica de Vehiculos (ITV)*.

⇒ Residence permit (NIE or NIF) with a photocopy.

⇒ Payment of the fee in cash, about Eur.35 to Eur.40 at time of printing.

⇒ You must also advise your local town hall (*ayuntimiento*) where the "road tax" is paid, of the change by completing their form, which de-registers your ownership with them.

⇒ Accept only **cash** or confirmed (by your bank) bank transfer for the car from the buyer before releasing the vehicle.

⇒ Take all this information to the *Trafico*, with a self-addressed and stamped envelope, for them to send you the finished documents, or, arrange for collection, as soon as possible.

⇒ Do not forget to advise your insurance company of the change and obtain a credit for any unused months of cover, if possible. Usually the credit is used for the insurance premium for the new vehicle. If you do not re-insure with the same broker / company, you may lose the unused balance.

If you no longer have the *permiso de circulacion* permit and the inspection certificate (*ITV* or MOT) because they are with the new owner, you can make out a sworn declaration to this effect with a Spanish notary (*gestoria* or *abogado*).

You may also carry out this act when you scrap an old car which, if not done, may be rebuilt and operated by someone else with the same financial consequences as described above.

PART 11-1

LIVING IN SPAIN, TEMPORARILY OR PERMANENTLY.

As with any other country, to live in Spain **permanently** without any strings attached, you have to take out citizenship. However, if you are a citizen of the EU, you can effectively remain here for ever (or until the Law changes) by renewing your *residencia* permit every five years. Until 2003, non-Spanish EU residents up to and from 6-months' stays, had to take out one of two documents. From March 1st 2003, however, the Law changed (Royal decree 178/2003). It applies only to EU member State nationals only, including Iceland, Lichenstein, and Norway and the Swiss confederation.

There is a book that covers this subject and much more such as buying and owning property in Spain, starting a business, etc., called "**You and the Law in Spain**", by David Searl. ISBN Number 84-89954-25-9. If you are coming to live in Spain, it is suggested that this book complements the book you are now reading and both will cover 99% of your needs here.

The book, like this one, is available in the UK at **amazon.co.uk**, as well as other leading book stores who have counters or displays for books on Spain.

IMPORTANT.

The Laws are always being updated, and this book is to be rewritten every year to include any changes or additions.

To ensure that readers are kept up to date until the next edition is published (usually about April each year), there are ongoing updates on my web site at: -

www.spainvia.com/motoringinspain.htm

The pages cover two months each, and it is recommended that you read each and every page to cover all topics. We wish you safe and happy motoring in Spain.

LATE ADDITIONS OF INTEREST.

Motorhomes, and commercial vehicles with right hand drive.

New residents with large vehicles with right-hand drive configuration (driven from the UK & Ireland, etc.) will NOT be able to change these vehicles onto Spanish registration. The reason is that the Spanish authorities have determined that due to problems with all round vision by the driver, they constitute a road safety hazard. This includes commercial vehicles such as vans and trucks. So it is better to either sell it before you come, or buy one with a left-hand drive. The decision is based on the reports on the causes after road accidents involving these vehicles.

Personalised Number Plates.
The Spanish licensing authorities do not allow personalised vehicle number-plates other than those especial to embassies, etc.

Register of Car Rental companies' debtors.
The national association of car rental companies has created a register of bad debtors, that is, those who do not pay their bills, and this is to be displayed on their web site. Special permission has been legally granted, effective from Easter week, even though under the EU Data Protection Act, it would otherwise be illegal. This includes those who do not pay traffic-fines, the customer's details being sent on the the police authority charging the customer.

Use of car emergency flashing lights.
It is now recognised and legal that in the event of traffic in front, or a road blockage, etc. causing you to slow down quickly, **it is expected** that you will activate the emergency flashers on your car, thus warning the drivers behind until it is obvious that they have seen the danger and slowed down.

Cyclists have priority on roundabouts.
Vehicle drivers are to give way to cyclists on a roundabout whether or not they are riding from your left or right. Also, in the proximity of cyclists, drivers and moto riders are to moderate driving so as not to endanger the passage of cyclists.

identities and of the facts which will speed up the settlement of claims.

| 1. **date** of accident | time | 2. **place** (exact location of accident) | 3. **injuries** even if slight |
| | | | no [ ]   yes [ ] * |

4. property damage other than to the vehicles A and B
no [ ]   yes [ ] *

5. witnesses names, addresses and tel. nos. (to be underlined if it relates to passenger in A or B)

vehicle A

6. insured policyholder *(see insurance cert.)*

Name (capital letters)
First name

Address

Tel. No. *(from 9 hrs. to 17 hrs.)*
Can the insured recover the Value Added Tax
on the vehicle?   no [ ]   yes [ ]

7. vehicle

Make, type

Registration No. (or engine No.)

8. insurance company

Policy No.

Agent (or broker)

Green Card No. *(if issued)*

Ins Cert. or } valid until
Green Card }

Is damage to the vehicle insured?
no [ ]   yes [ ]

9. driver *(see driving licence)*

12. circumstances
Put a cross (X) in each of the relevant spaces to help explain the plan.

parked (at the roadside)	1
leaving a parking place (at the roadside)	2
entering a parking place (at the roadside)	3
emerging from a car park, from private grounds, from a track	4
entering a car park, private grounds, a track	5
entering a roundabout (or similar traffic system)	6
circulating in a roundabout etc.	7
striking the rear of the other vehicle while going in the same direction and in the same lane	8
going in the same direction but in a different lane	9
changing lanes	10
overtaking	11
turning to the right	12
turning to the left	13

vehicle B

6. insured policyholder *(see insurance cert.)*

Name (capital letters)
First name

Address

Tel. No. *(from 9 hrs. to 17 hrs.)*
Can the insured recover the Value Added Tax
on the vehicle?   no [ ]   yes [ ]

7. vehicle

Make, type

Registration No. (or engine No.)

8. insurance company

Policy No.

Agent (or broker)

Green Card No. *(if issued)*

Ins Cert. or } valid until
Green Card }

Is damage to the vehicle insured?
no [ ]   yes [ ]

9. driver *(see driving licence)*

9. driver *(see driving licence)*

Name
(capital letters)
First name

Address

Driving licence No. _____ Issued by _____
Groups _____

valid from _____ to _____

	13		14

13	turning to the left	14	reversing
14		15	encroaching in the opposite traffic lane
15		16	coming from the right (at road junctions)
16		17	not observing a right of way sign
17			

➡ State TOTAL number of ➡
spaces marked with a cross

10. indicate by an arrow the point of initial impact

11. visible damage

13. plan of the accident

Indicate: 1. the layout of the road - 2. by arrows the direction of the vehicles A, B- 3. their position at the time of impact - 4. the road signs - 5. names of the streets or roads

14 remarks

9. driver *(see driving licence)*

Name
(capital letters)
First name

Address

Driving licence No. _____ Issued by _____
Groups _____

valid from _____ to _____

10. indicate by an arrow the point of initial impact

11. visible damage

15. signatures of the drivers

A

B

14 remarks

142

Insured

1. Occupation (if more than one state all)

Insured Vehicle

2. Make/Model/Type	C.C.	If commercial vehicle state carrying capacity and g.p.w.	Date of first registration as new	Registration mark

3. Please give/confirm instructions on my/our behalf (where appropriate) for the repairs

Are you the Owner? Yes ☐ No ☐   If no, state Owner's name and address

4. Exact purpose for which vehicle was being used at time of accident

5. Is the vehicle still in use? Yes ☐ No ☐   If no, state where it is at present

Tel. No. _____

6. Name and address of Finance Company (if any)

Driver or Person In charge of Vehicle

(If the Insured complete this section as appropriate)

7. Date of Birth	Occupation (if more than one, state all)	Date driving test passed	Was he driving with your permission?		Was he your employee?	
			Yes	No	Yes	No

8. Give details of any impairment of sight or hearing and of any other disability

9. Full details of all driving convictions including pending prosecutions

Date	Offence	Penalty

Injured Persons

10. Name(s), Address(es) and approximate Age(s)	Injuries Sustained	If Vehicle Occupants state in which vehicle	Were seat belts being worn?

143

Injured Persons				

	11 Owner(s) Name(s) and Address(es)	**Details of Vehicle or Property**	**Nature of Damage**	**Insurer's Name and Address (if known)**
Damage to Property & Vehicles (other than vehicles 'A' & 'B' overleaf)				

Police Action

12 Was the accident reported to Police   [Yes]   [No]

If yes, give station and P.C's name and number _____

13 Was warning of prosecution given?   [Yes]   [No]

If yes against whom? _____

Accident Details

14 Weather Conditions _____

15 Speed of vehicles   A [ ]   B [ ]

16 What warnings were given by driver or other party? _____

17 Were street lights illuminated?   [Yes]   [No]

18 What lights were displayed on your vehicle/the other vehicle(s)? _____

19 If your vehicle is commercial state weight of load carried at time of accident _____

20 State how accident happened, indicating width of roads, speed limits, etc. _____

144